WEEKNIGHT SMOKING

ON YOUR TRAEGER®

AND OTHER PELLET GRILLS

WEEKNIGHT SMOKING
ON YOUR TRAEGER®
AND OTHER PELLET GRILLS

Incredible
**WOOD-FIRED MEALS MADE
FAST AND EASY**

ADAM M^cKENZIE
founder of THIS JEW CAN QUE

PAGE STREET
PUBLISHING CO.

Copyright © 2021 Adam McKenzie

First published in 2021 by

Page Street Publishing Co.

27 Congress Street, Suite 105

Salem, MA 01970

www.pagestreetpublishing.com

Distributed by Macmillan, sales in Canada by The Canadian Manda Group.

25   24   23   22   21   1   2   3   4   5

ISBN-13: 978-1-64567-300-2

ISBN-10: 1-64567-300-6

Library of Congress Control Number: 2020948793

Cover and book design by Rosie Stewart for Page Street Publishing Co.

Photography by Ken Goodman

Photo on page 169 by Jackie Gragert

Printed and bound in the United States

To my wife, Isabel, for making this BBQ dream a reality. For letting Traegering become part of our lives and taking on all the challenges that have come with it. Sometimes that means waiting to eat because a picture needs to be taken first, eating at random hours because BBQ is done when it is done or waking up at 4:30 a.m. to drive an hour and a half to go eat legendary Texas BBQ. This journey is crazy and fun, and I wouldn't want anyone else on this adventure with me. Without you, none of this would be possible or as much fun.

CONTENTS

FOREWORD

Every once in a while, something will stop you in your tracks. This time it was a photo of a juicy, perfectly smoked brisket. I made my first connection with Adam the same way thousands of others have—through a mouthwatering photo he posted on Instagram. But I came to realize as our friendship grew in the ensuing years that it wasn't just the photos of food that draw you to Adam; it's his passion. A passion for crafting delicious food and, more importantly, for feeding others. Adam will often describe what he does as just cooking for his family and friends and sharing some photos and videos in the process, but his ability to connect with a community, locally and even worldwide, makes it that much more impactful. Behind every photo or video you'll find a story, maybe a catchy song or even a few pointers on that day's masterpiece. It's not just about showing off the food; it's about sharing an experience.

It's no surprise that, as an elementary schoolteacher, Adam is a natural at building a positive influence in the lives of others. He has managed to transform a backyard passion into a platform to connect with and educate countless others, inspiring them to cook more, do more and spend a little more time with those who matter most. Our core value at Traeger is bringing people together, and there are few out there who do as well as Adam. Whether they're his neighbors and friends, fellow Traeger owners or simply anyone who shares his passion for cooking outdoors, everyone is welcome at Adam's table.

It's fitting that the next step in Adam's journey is to create something to further educate and inspire the tight-knit, BBQ-loving community he's helped to foster. As you cook your way through this book, I have no doubt you'll find yourself better than when you started. And I can guarantee you'll pick up a lot more friends in the process. I couldn't be more impressed with the work Adam has done, and I'm excited to dig in and re-create these recipes at home for my own family and friends for years to come.

Thanks for making the world a more flavorful place, Adam.

JEREMY ANDRUS
CEO, Traeger Grills

INTRODUCTION

Congratulations! You are part of the Traeger family, and I couldn't be more excited that you chose to pick up my cookbook. If you've gotten this far, you probably have your Traeger grill set up and have maybe cooked a few things. It's amazing, isn't it? The first few cooks can be a challenge, but with some practice, you will soon get it dialed in, and I expect that you will want to start cooking all your meals on your Traeger grill, just as I did, even on your busiest weeknights.

It's not just about BBQ. With your Traeger, you can also grill, smoke, braise, bake and roast. I guess that's why Traegering has become a verb—because Traegered food is the best around, and you will soon be delighting your family and friends with amazing home-cooked meals. And your neighbors will be hoping for an invitation to dinner . . . every single night.

In this book, my wife, Isabel, and I are sharing some of our favorite fast and easy Traegered recipes. We want you to see that grilling doesn't have to be a hobby reserved for the weekend. It's something you can easily include in your busy life for a weeknight meal. As an elementary schoolteacher, I know how wiped out you can be when you get home from work. I love that whipping up a grilled dinner on a weeknight with a Traeger is easy, fast, clean and fun. With the simple push of a button and a short start-up time—often faster than doing the prep itself—you can have amazing wood-fired flavor on the table in a matter of minutes. From traditional favorites like a whole roasted chicken (page 48) to Smash Burgers (page 39) and the perfect Reverse-Seared Steak (page 27), you'll find something that suits your appetite any day of the week.

Most recipes in this book can be completed in less than an hour, with a majority clocking in at about 30 minutes. Some may recommend marinating times for a few hours or overnight, but with a bit of planning, you can toss that together either the night before or in the morning before you leave for work, then fire up the grill when you walk in the door. After a few backyard cooks on a weeknight, I bet you'll be hooked and start finding excuses to use your grill nightly, like we do.

A special chapter of sped-up standards (page 93), like brisket, beef dino bones and pulled pork, is included to demonstrate that BBQing doesn't always have to be "low and slow" and take all day (or multiple days) to be great. Low(ish) and slow(ish) is the name of our game. Get a good smoky base, bump up the temp and get dinner on the table in less time. And of course, there are a few great appetizer, side and dessert recipes, so you can show your friends and family how an entire dinner can be cooked in your backyard. In the end, I hope you'll find inspiration and use these recipes as a launching point for your own Traegered delights.

Before we dive into an array of our tested and loved recipes, this book begins with a chapter to help you master your Traeger. I'll go into some detail on the techniques used throughout the book, share tips on the other tools that will make your cooking successful and provide some insight on selecting pellets, sourcing your proteins and rubs and choosing seasonings and sauces to jump-start your cooking. I recommend starting your journey at the beginning of this book because it will set the stage for the recipes and empower you with the knowledge to take your grilling to the next level.

As evidenced by the title, my focus in this book is cooking on Traeger grills, but the recipes apply to any brand of pellet grill. The procedure remains the same regardless of the grill you have, and most recipes can be cooked equally well in your oven when you don't have access to a grill.

I've found that perfectly cooked food happens with a little patience and a thermometer. The internal temperature of whatever you cook will signal the best finished results, so guidelines for time and the perfect finish temperatures are included throughout the recipes.

An important note is that I cook at high altitude—5,280 feet (1,609 m) above sea level in Denver, Colorado—where the air is very dry. As a result, cooking times are generally based on my own experience in this climate and at this altitude. If you're cooking somewhere humid or at a lower altitude, your cooks may go faster than what I have described in this book. And you're likely to end up with moister results if you are cooking at sea level, because the things you are grilling will lose less moisture during the cooking process. My recommendation is to keep a digital probe thermometer handy and check the internal temperatures of what you're cooking frequently. Every grill runs a little differently, but once you get a handle on how your grill runs, you'll get into a good rhythm regarding the length of time it takes to cook each dish.

My love of Traegering started humbly with the purchase of my first Tailgater at my local hardware store and quickly developed into a passion that has led to so many incredible friendships and amazing meals. Cooking at home is a joy these days, and I hope this collection of approachable and delicious recipes will inspire you as a Traeger home chef and bring you the same memorable family meals.

MASTERING YOUR
TRAEGER

One of my goals in writing this book was to give Traeger owners some ideas and resources to make cooking on the Traeger a part of their daily life. When we got our first Traeger—a Tailgater—we reserved it for "special" occasions and weekends when we had adequate time and energy to cook on the grill. But in hardly any time at all, it became something we used more and more often. My "little Tailgater that could" has cooked for probably a thousand hours and seen at least that many pounds of meat. Since then, we've expanded our Traeger arsenal to include one of each of Traeger's main models, and every single one is predictable, fun and produces great food. Now we've gone from being weekend warriors on the grill to cooking four to six nights a week on the grill. From baking eggplant parmesan to whipping up a perfectly reverse-seared steak, the versatility of the grill makes cooking at home really fun and ultimately pretty fast.

This chapter is intended to give you a quick overview of the models and pellets offered by Traeger, advice on sourcing your meat, the few tools I believe are must-haves for successful Traegering and information on some spices, rubs and sauces I recommend if you're not making your own. And, of course, I've outlined some common techniques in detail that are referenced throughout the recipes.

Note that while my focus is on Traeger pellet grills, much of this information applies to pellet smoker grills under other brand names. Each grill brand has unique features and capabilities, but generally speaking, they can cook at low temperatures with large amounts of smoke and also at higher temperatures for searing, fast cooking and more traditional grilling.

YOUR TRAEGER

Traeger offers a variety of grills that fit into most budgets. From the small and mighty Tailgater and Ranger to the WiFIRE models of Timberline, Ironwood and Pro. Regardless of the grill you have, you can make amazing food with that notable wood-fired flavor. All of the grills can produce low-temperature smoke (some with the Super Smoke mode) and each can reach at least 450°F (232°C).

While you may think that 450°F (232°C) isn't a very high temperature, the recipes in this book all come out fantastic at or below this temperature. In my experience, the benefit of a Traeger is the flavor, and you can sear wonderfully at 450°F (232°C), which is what seals in the flavor. A cast-iron griddle or pan can serve as a great superhot surface for all-over/flat searing. Or pick up a set of GrillGrates to add to your Traeger, which will help concentrate the heat to get those perfect diamond marks.

If you're lucky enough to have more than one Traeger, I recommend using one for slow/low cooking and one for cranking up the heat if you're reverse searing. But you certainly don't need two grills, and as long as you do a bit of planning, you can take a grill from 225°F (107°C) Super Smoke to searing hot in a matter of minutes. I don't have a favorite grill in the lineup—they are each unique—but they all have the same great features that produce delicious food.

PELLETS

In each recipe, I suggest pellets that you could use for your cook. The following chart provides a little more information on which Traeger-brand hardwood pellets are particularly suited for which proteins. My recommendation is to pick a versatile flavor—like signature, pecan or cherry—and use that most of the time. I find this easier than keeping track and emptying your hopper frequently. Any cooking under 275°F (135°C) will add a good amount of smoke flavor from the pellets to what you cook. Temperatures higher than that produce very little smoke, so the pellet flavor doesn't matter much.

RECOMMENDED PELLETS

PELLETS	GOOD FOR
Signature*	Beef, Chicken, Pork, Seafood, Vegetables
Pecan	Beef, Chicken, Pork, Vegetables
Cherry	Beef, Chicken, Pork
Apple	Chicken, Pork
Mesquite	Beef, Chicken, Seafood, Vegetables
Hickory	Beef, Chicken, Pork, Vegetables

*Signature is a pellet blend specific to Traeger that includes hickory, cherry and maple pellets. You can also get the same blend, under the moniker "gourmet," at Costco stores.

SOURCING YOUR PROTEINS

Cooking on a Traeger can make the simplest and most inexpensive meats taste delicious. Take, for example, the recipe for Chuck Roast Burnt Ends (page 98), or as I also like to call them, "Poor Man's Burnt Ends." A simple, inexpensive chuck roast is slow smoked and elevated into an amazing dish that your family and friends will love. As you're getting comfortable with your grill, you can absolutely use less expensive meats to perfect your techniques. Then, when you feel up to it, indulge in a more expensive cut, like a cowboy ribeye, and give it a reverse sear. Whoever is lucky enough to be there for dinner will be amazed.

To ensure we always have meat on hand to cook on my Traegers throughout the week, we source our meat from retailers that ship to our home. My beef and pork come from Snake River Farms/Double R Ranch and arrive individually frozen. Before I head out the door to work each day, I pop something in the fridge to defrost, and it makes cooking dinner at home in the evening really simple. The same goes for seafood and fish. I highly recommend stocking your freezer with things you can transform on your Traeger.

Some of my go-to delivery companies for proteins include:

- Snake River Farms (beef & pork)
- Fulton Fish Market (fish & seafood)
- Lobster Anywhere (lobster)
- Superior Farms (lamb)
- Red Bird Farms (chicken & turkey)
- Salmon & Sable (salmon)

TOOLS

Beyond the obvious of having a Traeger or pellet grill, there are a few items I highly recommend the avid griller have on hand.

DIGITAL PROBE THERMOMETER

If you are only buying one more thing after you get your Traeger, I implore you to buy a high-quality digital probe thermometer. ThermoWorks is my favorite brand. They are reliable, well-calibrated, compact and you can read the temperature instantly. The small probe doesn't cause a leaky hole in your meat, and nearly every recipe in this book includes guidance on cooking to temperature. The extra investment in a ThermoWorks thermometer will help you perfect smoking faster on the Traeger in no time.

CAST-IRON SKILLET, CAST-IRON GRIDDLE AND/OR GRILLGRATES

A Traeger grill is a workhorse and has a significant temperature range. However, some users struggle to get a great sear on their cooks using the Traeger alone. In my experience, if you give the grill time to fully preheat, a temperature setting of 450°F (232°C) can get you a great sear. But I've also found that using a superhot piece of cast iron (either a griddle or a skillet) or a set of GrillGrates can help concentrate the high heat and produce an excellent, reliable seared crust on hot and fast and reverse-seared cooks. GrillGrates are specialty aluminum additions to your grill that get really hot, resulting in fantastic grill marks. Throughout this cookbook, I mention using cast iron (either a griddle or skillet) or GrillGrates to get the ultimate sear. You don't need all of them—just one will work for a variety of dishes.

WOODEN CUTTING BOARD

A good-quality hardwood cutting board is a key part of making BBQ and grilled food. Get something large enough to hold the larger cuts you might cook. My favorite size is 15 x 20 inches (38 x 51 cm), and if it has a groove on one side, that's all the better. Maintain it with beeswax or mineral oil, and always dry it immediately after washing. Your knives will stay sharper with a good cutting board.

SEASONINGS & SAUCES

While there are many recipes for sauces, rubs and seasonings in this cookbook, I know from experience that sometimes time is of the essence when it comes to getting dinner on the table on a weeknight, and there are some great "shortcuts" that I recommend you have on hand. A couple of versatile spice blends are all you need. I'm, of course, partial to the four rub blends that I collaborated with Spiceology to create. However, the chart on the next page suggests some others you could try. I offer six recipes for homemade BBQ sauce toward the end of the book (see pages 158 to 161), but have recommended a few premade options in the following chart as well.

RECOMMENDED SEASONINGS & SAUCES

SEASONINGS FOR BEEF	SEASONINGS FOR POULTRY	SEASONINGS FOR PORK
Double Smoke by Spiceology	Double Smoke by Spiceology	Double Smoke by Spiceology
Garlic Junky by Spiceology	Spicy Bloody Mary by Spiceology	Honey Hog BBQ by Meat Church BBQ
Coffee Junky by Spiceology	Chicken Rub by Traeger	Old Fashioned by Whiskey Bent BBQ
Blackened Saskatchewan by Traeger	The Blazin' Bird by Whiskey Bent BBQ	Pork & Poultry by Traeger
The Rocks by Whiskey Bent BBQ		
Holy Cow by Meat Church BBQ		
GREAT ALL-PURPOSE SEASONINGS	**SEASONINGS FOR SEAFOOD**	**BBQ SAUCES**
Garlic Junky by Spiceology	Spicy Bloody Mary by Spiceology	Sweet Mamma by BurntOut BBQ Co.
Garlic Herb by Spiceology	Garlic Junky by Spiceology	Grill Candy by BurntOut BBQ Co.
Coffee Junky by Spiceology	Fin & Feather by Traeger	Apple Habanero by Head Country
Steak Seasoning by Jacobsen Salt Co.	Honey Hog BBQ by Meat Church BBQ	Original by Five Monkeys
	Seafood Seasoning by Jacobsen Salt Co.	

I also want to share a couple easy spice blends you can make at home, often with ingredients you already have in your pantry, to have on hand for weeknight cooking. Once you start experimenting with creating your own blends, the sky is the limit!

The method is the same for each of the blends. Combine all the ingredients and mix until well incorporated. Store for 6 months in the cupboard.

KILLER BEEF SEASONING

2 tbsp (28 g) kosher salt

3 tbsp (21 g) coarse ground black pepper (16 mesh)

2 tbsp (7 g) paprika

2 tbsp (20 g) garlic powder

1 tbsp (7 g) onion powder

1 tsp dried oregano

1 tsp cumin

1 tsp brown sugar

PERFECT PORK RUB

3 tbsp (40 g) brown sugar

2 tbsp (28 g) kosher salt

2 tbsp (14 g) coarse ground black pepper (16 mesh)

1 tsp paprika

1 tsp ground mustard

1 tsp garlic powder

1 tsp chili powder

¼ tsp cinnamon

CLASSIC CHICKEN BLEND

1 tbsp (14 g) kosher salt

1 tbsp (7 g) onion powder

1 tbsp (10 g) garlic powder

1 tbsp (3 g) paprika

1 tsp white pepper

1 tsp cayenne pepper

1 tsp coarse ground black pepper (16 mesh)

1 tsp dried thyme

TECHNIQUES

There are four main techniques that I use throughout this book: Hot & Fast, the Reverse Sear, Outdoor Oven and Low(ish) & Slow(ish). The purpose of this book is to help make using the Traeger more approachable to the everyday backyard grilling enthusiast. While there are times and purposes for each of the four techniques, my focus is on speeding things up, usually with a slightly higher temperature, so it's possible to get dinner on the table in a reasonable amount of time. And while every recipe gives you a guideline for cook time or total time, I truly believe that good BBQ takes time and is best cooked to temperature. So, the recommended times are to be used as guidelines; have your trusty digital probe thermometer on hand to help you get it dialed in perfectly.

As a reminder, these recipes were developed based on my experiences living at high altitude with dry air. Depending on where you live, your cook times may be a little faster than the estimates I've provided. Because there are so many variables with cooking, even on a Traeger, the key is using your digital probe thermometer to check the internal temperature of your food frequently and cooking to temperature rather than strictly according to the time estimates provided in the recipes.

HOT & FAST

Just as the name implies, this technique uses high heat (450°F [232°C] or more) and brief cook times. You'll get a great sear on the exterior of meats, and the interior will cook to a specifc internal temperature. For that reason, it's important to keep your digital probe thermometer on hand to moniter the temperature of what you're cooking (refer to the Finish Temperature Chart on page 20). When cooking hot and fast on the Traeger, your selection of pellets isn't important, as the amount of smoke produced in hot cooks is negligible. I generally just use whatever is in my pellet hopper from the last cook. This technique is great for burgers, thin cuts like flank steak, skirt steak and Korean-style short ribs. Thicker steaks and roasts don't lend themselves well to hot and fast cooking, and I recommend a reverse sear for these cuts to get the most tender, juicy and flavorful results.

THE REVERSE SEAR

A variety of proteins can be reverse seared—especially beef, pork, lamb and wild game. This technique will help you serve your family steaks, roasts and chops that are the perfect temperature, without any pockets of undercooked meat in the center and dried-out meat on the edges. A reverse sear takes a bit longer than a traditional sear, but I promise that the results are worth it.

The idea is simple—cook your meat slowly at first in a smoke bath to impart amazing wood-fired flavor and edge-to-edge temperature perfection. Then, once the internal temperature of the meat is about 10 to 15°F (2 to 4°C) shy of the target internal temperature, you crank up the heat to get an amazing crust and/or grill marks and seal in the flavor and juices. With this method, you don't even need to rest your meat before cutting it, as the juices have had the opportunity to be distributed throughout the meat during the entire cook.

If you are crunched for time, you can cut corners a bit to speed up the reverse-sear process. Rather than starting the cook at 225°F (107°C), which will provide great smoke flavor, you could begin cooking the meat at 275°F (135°C) instead. You'll get a little less smoke flavor, but it will still be delicious. If you do start the cook at a higher temperature, the cook time will decrease by about 25 percent. Keep an eye on the internal temperature with your digital probe thermometer until you perfect this cooking technique.

Here are the basic instructions for a perfectly reverse-seared steak:

1. Select your desired steak for the cook. The time it will take for your steak to reach the near-done internal temperature will largely depend on the thickness of the cut, but I've found that this technique works particularly well with big cuts like a tomahawk steak, which can be 2 to 4 inches (5 to 10 cm) thick.

2. Use a high-quality oil to coat the steak, then apply your rub or seasoning of choice.

3. Fill your grill's pellet hopper with the pellets of your choice. Your steak will get a smoke bath as it cooks, so my preference is something like pecan, cherry or apple, which imparts a great flavor.

4. Preheat your Traeger grill to 225°F (107°C) with the lid closed and turn on the Super Smoke feature if your grill has it. Place a cast-iron griddle, cast-iron skillet or GrillGrates in the grill to heat up.

5. When the grill has preheated, place your seasoned steak directly on the grates in the center of the grill and close the lid.

6. Allow the steak to cook for about 20 minutes, then begin checking the internal temperature at the center of the steak with a digital probe thermometer. There is no need to flip the meat during this step, as it is getting even heat from the Traeger's convection-style cooking. Also, you don't need to remove the steak to check the temperature—just insert the probe into the middle of the steak, and you'll get an instant temperature reading. Use the Finish Temperature Chart to the right to determine the temperature at which you should remove the steak from the grill. Keep an eye on the internal temperature of the steak as it gets close to the pull temperature—remember that you want to remove the steak about 10 to 15°F (2 to 4°C) before it reaches the final desired internal temperature, since it will continue cooking during the final sear. I recommend checking the temperatures after the first 20 minutes, then every 8 to 10 minutes thereafter.

7. When the steak has reached the pull temperature, transfer the steak to a plate or cutting board and tent it loosely with aluminum foil.

8. Turn up the heat on your Traeger to its highest temperature setting (on most models this would be 450°F [232°C]), and allow it to get really hot for about 10 minutes.

9. When the grill has reached its highest temperature, place your steak on the hot griddle, skillet or GrillGrates that's been inside the grill. Close the lid and cook for about 90 seconds per side, rotating once halfway through to achieve great diamond grill marks if you're using a surface with ridges. Flip over and repeat.

10. Transfer the steak to a cutting board and use a sharp knife to cut it against the grain for everyone to enjoy—and hope you end up with leftovers for tomorrow!

If you want to get deep into the science of the reverse sear, I highly recommend The Food Lab blog on SeriousEats.com, where chef J. Kenji López-Alt shares the secrets behind the method.

FINISH TEMPERATURE CHART

PULL TEMPERATURE, THEN SEAR FOR 3–5 MINUTES	FINAL TEMPERATURE	FINISH TEMPERATURES FOR MEAT
105–115°F (41–46°C)	120–125°F (49–52°C)	Beef: Rare Lamb: Rare
115–130°F (46–54°C)	130–140°F (54–60°C)	Beef: Medium rare Lamb: Medium rare
130–135°F (54–57°C)	145°F (63°C)	Beef: Medium Lamb: Medium Pork: Medium rare Fish & Shellfish: Cooked through
135–140°F (57–60°C)	150°F (66°C)	Beef: Medium well Lamb: Medium well Pork: Medium
145–150°F (63–66°C)	160°F (71°C)	Beef: Well Lamb: Well Pork: Well
150–155°F (66–68°C)	165°F (74°C)	Chicken: Cooked through Turkey: Cooked through
n/a	195°F (91°C)	Beef: Shredded (chuck roast)
n/a	204°F (96°C)	Pork: Shredded Beef: Tender for slicing (brisket)

OUTDOOR OVEN

As the name implies, these recipes are more along the lines of traditional baking than backyard grilling. It's not so much about the smoke that flavors the meat, and the cook times are reflective of traditional oven baking times. This category could easily be called "baking" if it were a cookbook for an indoor oven. A whole roasted chicken, a portion of salmon and a pan of brownies all fit in this category. These cooks all benefit from the even convection heat of your Traeger and will give your oven in the kitchen a (perhaps permanent?) break.

LOW(ISH) & SLOW(ISH)

While this book focuses on easy, accessible Traegering during the week, I wanted to provide a chapter of more traditional BBQ recipes for you to try. Very traditional BBQ swears by the low and slow technique—cooking meats at the lowest temperatures possible for many, many hours. Doing a low and slow cook in the Traeger is far easier than if you were cooking in a stick burner smoker. The generous pellet hopper and auger ensure an even, consistent heat throughout your cook. However, the low and slow technique is impractical for many of us with jobs and families and other obligations.

For this cookbook, I have sped up some of the iconic low and slow recipes, such as pork shoulder, brisket, beef ribs, etc., to better economize your time and help you get dinner on the table faster. They are cooked low(ish) and slow(ish), meaning you'll end up with the same smoky, tender and flavorful results, but you won't have to wait as long for the food to finish cooking. As you will see in this book, many of the longer-cook recipes call for a smoke bath (at temperatures around 225°F [107° C]) to kick off the cooking, then the temperature is bumped up (to about 350°F [177°C]) to speed things along. Once you've done it a few times, your dinner guests will be impressed by your brisket cooked in 7 hours rather than 17, and they will not be able to tell the difference. I recommend trying these cooks out on a weekend day, as you may need up to 8 hours (including rest time) for most of them, and as you get familiar with the recipes, you can adjust the cooks to best suit your interests.

When you are getting close to that finished temperature in Low(ish) & Slow(ish) cooks, start checking for probe tenderness. You can do this by sliding your temperature probe into the meat and feeling how much resistance you are getting. A perfectly probe-tender cook will have little resistance and will feel like pushing a knife through room-temperature butter. If you feel resistance when checking probe tenderness, give the cook a little more time to render.

If you want to achieve a smokier flavor in whatever you're cooking, you can extend the smoke bath portion of the cook before bumping up the temperature. As always, use a digital probe thermometer to monitor the internal temperature of your cooks, as the time will likely be lengthened a bit. Either way, your cooks will come out fantastic, and you can delight your family with some amazing traditional(ish) BBQ.

QUICK-SMOKED
STEAKS
& BURGERS

Before I got my Traeger grill, a quick grilled dinner after work was often frozen-beef-patties-turned-hamburgers or an occasional steak that was too rare in the middle and quite overdone on the outside. Life with a Traeger has resulted in different and much tastier dinners at our house. This chapter provides recipes that can level up your grilling game to help you transition from boring to amazing, even on your busiest nights. These recipes can be cooked quickly, and they provide a lot of versatility. Most are done in a matter of minutes, with a handful of exceptions that are closer to an hour, but still worth the extra bit of time for their spectacular smoked flavor. Switch up the seasonings and marinades and pair them with a different side and sauce from this book, and you'll have a different, delicious dinner every night.

MARINATED SKIRT STEAK

COOK TIME
10 minutes (plus at least
30 minutes to marinate and
10 minutes to rest)

YIELD
4 servings

PELLET
Any

TECHNIQUE
Hot & Fast (page 19)

EQUIPMENT
Shallow glass baking dish
with a cover (or plastic wrap),
for marinating

MARINADE
¼ cup (60 ml) soy sauce

2 tbsp (30 ml) olive oil

2 tbsp (30 ml) Worcestershire
sauce

¼ cup (60 ml) hot sauce

2 tbsp (28 g) brown sugar

2 tbsp (30 ml) rice wine
vinegar

¼ cup (60 ml) Dijon mustard

4 garlic cloves, minced

Red pepper flakes

STEAK
1 (1-lb [454-g]) skirt steak,
trimmed

Corn & Poblano Salsa
(page 164), for serving
(optional)

Marinating steak is a terrific way to impart lots of flavor in a short amount of time. We recommend that you marinate your cut overnight or for a few hours, but if you're crunched for time, 30 minutes should do. With a bit of planning, we try to prep the marinade for a steak like this before we leave for work/school. Pop it in the fridge, covered, and when you get home in the evening, bring it back to room temperature while you preheat the grill.

This steak recipe calls for a hot and fast technique, which cooks the steak in about ten minutes. Give yourself a few minutes to rest the meat after cooking and slice it thinly against the grain for best results. You can apply this recipe and technique to any type of steak—we especially like flank, skirt and flat iron steaks.

Combine the soy sauce, olive oil, Worcestershire sauce, hot sauce, brown sugar, vinegar, mustard and garlic in a bowl. Whisk well and season with red pepper flakes to taste. Cut the skirt steak into even 8-inch (20-cm)-long pieces. A full skirt steak should make three or four 8-inch (20-cm) pieces. Place the steak in a glass baking dish. Pour the marinade over the steak, turning the pieces to coat them evenly. Cover the baking dish and place it in the fridge for at least 30 minutes, but preferably an hour or more, and up to 24 hours.

Preheat your Traeger grill to 450°F (232°C), and allow it to heat up for at least 15 minutes with the lid closed. Remove the steak from the marinade, and pat it dry with a paper towel. This will allow the meat to sear really well and produce a great crust. Discard the marinade.

Place the meat in the center of the preheated grill, and sear for about 3 minutes per side, rotating 45 degrees while cooking to create diamond grill marks.

Transfer the steak to a cutting board, and allow it to rest, tented loosely in foil, for 10 minutes. Slice against the grain and serve with the salsa if desired.

FAST HACK! A basic marinade like this can be adjusted with whatever ingredients you have on hand. You can use balsamic vinegar in place of the rice wine vinegar or add sesame oil for an Asian-style flavor. A little acid, something salty and a touch of sweet make for a great base. Experiment and see what your family likes best!

REVERSE-SEARED STEAK

COOK TIME
35–50 minutes (plus
5 minutes to rest)

YIELD
2–4 servings

PELLET
Signature

TECHNIQUE
Reverse Sear (page 19)

EQUIPMENT
Cast-iron skillet, griddle or
GrillGrates
Digital probe thermometer

INGREDIENTS
2 tsp (10 ml) olive oil

1 (10–16-ounce [283–454-g],
1-inch [2.5-cm]-thick) steak,
such as a bone-in ribeye

3 tbsp (39 g) steak seasoning,
such as Garlic Junky by
Spiceology

Chimichurri (page 165), for
serving (optional)

Cooking a steak hot and fast has its advantages, but the reverse sear will get you a perfect cook every time. After you cook a steak this way, you will be hooked on the technique. A reverse sear works perfectly for those larger cuts like tri-tip and cowboy ribeyes, but it is fantastic for just about any steak. The idea behind this method is to first build delicious smoke flavor from the wood-fired grill, then create an amazing crust at the end. Refer to the Finish Temperature Chart on page 20 to determine when to pull the steak off the grill.

Preheat your Traeger grill to 225°F (107°C), and turn on the Super Smoke feature if your grill has it. Place a cast-iron skillet in the grill to heat up.

While the grill preheats, apply a thin layer of olive oil over the steak on all sides. Then apply the seasoning to the steak, making sure to cover the edges and both sides.

When the grill is hot, place the steak in the center of the grill, and allow it to cook slowly to ensure a consistent edge-to-edge cook. You want the steak to reach an internal temperature that is within 10 to 15°F (5 to 8°C) of your desired finished temperature. For a medium-rare finished steak (125 to 130°F [51 to 54°C]), cook the steak to around 115°F (46°C).

The timing of this process depends on the thickness of the steak. After about 20 minutes on the grill, check the steak's temperature with a digital probe thermometer, then monitor the temperature every 10 minutes. A 1-inch (2.5-cm)-thick steak will generally take about 30 to 45 minutes to reach your first benchmark temperature.

When the steak hits the benchmark temperature, transfer it to a cutting board and tent it with foil. Increase the temperature of your grill to 500°F (260°C) for searing. Once the grill reaches 500°F (260°C), sear the steak in the superhot cast-iron skillet for about 2 minutes on each side. Check the internal temperature again, and remove the steak from the skillet about 5°F (3°C) below your target temperature of 125 to 130°F (51 to 54°C). Allow the steak to rest for about 5 minutes, and slice it against the grain. Spoon the chimmichurri on top, if using, and enjoy.

FAST HACK! A tasty variation on this recipe is to butter baste the steak during the final sear. To do so, heat up a cast-iron skillet inside your grill, then place the steak directly in the skillet to sear. Cook for about 90 seconds on one side, then flip the steak over. When you flip it over, add 2 to 3 tablespoons (30 to 45 g) of a compound butter (such as Garlic Junky Compound Butter on page 162) to the skillet. Using a big spoon, carefully ladle the melted butter over the steak repeatedly while it cooks for another 90 seconds or so. Check the internal temperature of the steak after about 90 seconds per side, and when the steak has reached your desired temperature, transfer it to a cutting board to briefly rest before serving.

COLORADO TRI-TIP WITH SANTA MARIA SALSA

COOK TIME
40 minutes (plus 15 minutes to rest)

YIELD
4-6 servings

PELLET
Pecan or hickory

TECHNIQUE
Reverse Sear (page 19)

EQUIPMENT
Digital probe thermometer

SANTA MARIA SALSA
2 large ripe tomatoes, diced
2 celery ribs, diced
2 scallions, chopped
2 roasted green chiles, diced
¼ cup (8 g) chopped cilantro
2 garlic cloves, minced
2 tbsp (30 ml) red wine vinegar
1 tbsp (15 ml) olive oil
1 tbsp (15 ml) Worcestershire sauce
1 tsp cumin
Kosher salt
Freshly ground black pepper

STEAK
1 (about 3-lb [1.3-kg]) tri-tip roast
½ cup (66 g) beef rub, such as Coffee Junky from Spiceology

Tri-tip is one of our favorite cuts of steak to cook. Tri-tip comes from the lower part of the bottom sirloin on the cow. It has lots of marbling and is a tender cut of beef. It can be somewhat hard to find, so I recommend ordering from an online butcher if you are having trouble sourcing it in your local stores. A tri-tip is delicious when reverse seared, and we like to serve it with a crunchy Santa Maria-style salsa, which is a little spicy, savory and has a great texture because of the unexpected ingredient of finely chopped celery. The salsa can be prepared while you cook the steak, or ahead of time and refrigerated until you're ready to serve. Give it a try!

To make the Santa Maria salsa, in a medium bowl, combine the tomatoes, celery, scallions, green chiles, cilantro, garlic, vinegar, olive oil, Worcestershire sauce and cumin and mix well. Season with salt and pepper to taste. Cover and refrigerate for at least 15 minutes.

Preheat your Traeger grill to 250°F (121°C). While the grill is heating up, prep the tri-tip by trimming away some of the hard fat. You can also trim the silver skin from the roast. Season the meat liberally with the rub. It is a large cut and can take a lot of seasoning.

Place the tri-tip in the center of the grill and cook for about 20 minutes. Begin checking the internal temperature every 10 to 15 minutes until it reaches 120°F (49°C). It should take about 35 minutes for the meat to hit the benchmark temperature.

When the meat reaches 120°F (49°C), transfer it to a cutting board and tent it with foil. Increase the temperature of your grill to 450°F (232°C) for searing. Once the grill reaches 450°F (232°C), sear the tri-tip on the grill for about 2 minutes on each side. Remove the tri-tip from the grill when the internal temperature reaches 130°F (54°C) for medium rare. Let the meat rest for 15 minutes before slicing. Remove the salsa from the fridge and taste it again to see if you want to adjust the seasonings. Serve the sliced steak with the salsa.

FAST HACK! Before you cut the tri-tip, identify the grain in the meat. It will go in three directions (hence the name), and you'll want to adjust your slicing to ensure you are always slicing against the grain. Cut the tri-tip in half where the grain changes directions, then slice each half according to (and against) the grain direction. Check out the picture to see how we sliced the roast from all three points. Your dinner guests will be really happy with this dish, as the ends will be more medium and the middle will be closer to rare. All your diners will find slices that make them happy.

SMOKED KOREAN-STYLE SHORT RIBS

COOK TIME
15 minutes (plus at least 1 hour to marinate)

YIELD
4 servings

PELLET
Any

TECHNIQUE
Hot & Fast (page 19)

EQUIPMENT
Large bowl or shallow glass baking dish with a cover (or plastic wrap), for marinating

Cast-iron griddle or large cast-iron skillet

INGREDIENTS
6 tbsp (75 g) white sugar

6 tbsp (90 ml) soy sauce

6 tbsp (90 ml) apple juice

¼ cup (60 ml) sesame oil

2 garlic cloves, minced

4 tbsp (56 g) minced fresh ginger

½ tbsp (7 ml) water

2 lbs (908 g), cross-cut, bone-in short ribs, ½ inch (1.3 cm) thick

Cooking oil spray

2 cups (400 g) cooked sticky white rice

Sesame seeds, for serving

Thinly sliced green onions, for serving

This is my favorite way to cook Korean short ribs on the grill. Cooking them hot and fast produces delicious caramelized edges, and the marinade ensures you end up with tender and juicy meat. I recommend preparing the ribs in the marinade before you leave for work, which will make cooking dinner super quick when you get home. See the Fast Hack below about sourcing this cut of beef.

In a large bowl or shallow glass baking dish, combine the sugar, soy sauce, apple juice, sesame oil, garlic, ginger and water and mix well. Place the beef in the marinade, and mix with your hands until each piece is coated in sauce. Cover and refrigerate for about 1 hour, or up to overnight.

Preheat your Traeger grill to 450°F (232°C). Place a cast-iron griddle in the grill, and allow the grill to heat up for at least 20 minutes with the lid closed.

When you're ready to cook, remove the meat from the marinade, and gently pat each piece dry with paper towels. Discard the marinade. Spray the preheated griddle with cooking oil spray. Then cook the beef in batches, searing 2 to 3 minutes per side until a good crust has developed.

Place the cooked ribs on a platter or tray, tent them loosely with foil and cook the remaining batches. Serve them immediately with rice, and sprinkle with sesame seeds and green onions for garnish.

FAST HACK! You want to get this specific cut of beef to achieve the best results. We've found them advertised differently depending on where we shop. Flanken-style short ribs are what they are commonly called. They are thin-cut slices of meat, including little discs of the bone, from your traditional BBQ-focused beef short rib. Essentially, the bones are cut across rather than being cut apart. We usually find them in packages of 10 to 20, with three to four bone discs per slice and a thickness of about ½ inch (1.3 cm). The cut includes meat interspersed with muscle, fat and tendon, which makes for a strong beefy flavor. Sometimes they're called *kalbi*. They could also be advertised as English cut, but those are 2 to 3 inches (5 to 8 cm) thick, cut in the same cross-bone direction. Ask your butcher if you need help!

FESTIVAL FLANK STEAK SANDWICHES

COOK TIME

15 minutes (plus at least 30 minutes to marinate and 10 minutes to rest)

YIELD

4 sandwiches

PELLET

Any

TECHNIQUE

Hot & Fast (page 19)

EQUIPMENT

Gallon-sized zip-top bag for marinating

Cast-iron skillet

Digital probe thermometer

INGREDIENTS

½ cup (120 ml) soy sauce

½ cup (120 ml) Worcestershire sauce

½ cup (120 ml) water

3 tbsp (30 g) garlic powder

1 (2-lb [908-g]) flank steak, trimmed

2 red, orange or yellow bell peppers, cut into strips

1 white onion, cut into strips

1 tbsp (15 ml) cooking oil

4 soft sandwich rolls

Sriracha sauce (optional)

These sandwiches are a family favorite. Every summer we spend a bit of time in Colorado's mountains while attending the Telluride Bluegrass Festival. All the festival food is tasty, but the "Killer Flank Steak Sandwiches" are especially good. This is our backyard take on their secret recipe, cooking the flank steak hot and fast on the Traeger. Be sure to slice the meat super thinly and against the grain, which will make eating it without a fork and knife easier! Serve with a drizzle of sriracha if you're feeling spicy. Best accompanied by a cold beer and good music.

In a medium bowl, combine the soy sauce, Worcestershire sauce, water and garlic powder. Pour all but ¼ cup (60 ml) of the mixture into a gallon-sized zip-top bag. Set the reserved marinade aside. Add the flank steak to the bag and allow it to marinate for at least 30 minutes, and up to 12 hours.

Preheat your Traeger grill to 450°F (232°C). Place a cast-iron skillet in the grill to heat up.

Once the grill is preheated, add the peppers, onion and cooking oil to the cast-iron skillet, and sauté for about 10 minutes, until softened. Stir in the reserved marinade, and cook for 5 more minutes, until the sauce thickens. Set aside.

While the veggies are cooking, remove the steak from the marinade, and pat it dry with paper towels. Discard the marinade. Place the steak directly on the grill, allowing it to cook for 2 to 3 minutes on each side. Rotate the meat 90 degrees while cooking to create diamond grill marks. Remove the steak from the grill when the internal temperature reaches 130°F (54°C) for medium rare. Transfer the steak to a cutting board and allow it to rest, tented loosely in foil, for 10 minutes.

Thinly slice the meat against the grain. Assemble the sandwiches by piling meat on a split sandwich roll. Top with the peppers and onions and drizzle with the sriracha, if desired.

WOOD-FIRED CARNE ASADA

This flavorful marinated steak is perfect for tacos, burritos or just eating right off the cutting board. Serve it with warm tortillas, fresh salsa, grilled jalapeños, scallions and lime wedges for an amazing dinner that cooks in only 15 minutes. Drop the steak in the marinade in the morning, and it'll be perfect to make a quick weeknight dinner on the grill.

COOK TIME
15 minutes (plus at least 2 hours to marinate and 10 minutes to rest)

YIELD
4–6 servings

PELLET
Any

TECHNIQUE
Hot & Fast (page 19)

EQUIPMENT
Shallow glass baking dish with a cover (or plastic wrap), for marinating

Digital probe thermometer

INGREDIENTS
2 tbsp (12 g) ground cumin

2 tbsp (20 g) garlic powder

2 tsp (5 g) paprika

1 tsp kosher salt

1 tsp chili powder

1 tsp onion powder

1 tsp freshly ground black pepper

½ tsp cayenne pepper

½ cup (120 ml) orange juice

Juice of ½ a lime

Juice of ½ a lemon

¼ cup (60 ml) soy sauce

2 tbsp (30 ml) olive oil

2 garlic cloves, minced

1 jalapeño, diced

2 thin-cut ribeye steaks (about 1½–2 lbs [680–908 g] total)

In a shallow glass baking dish, combine the ground cumin, garlic powder, paprika, salt, chili powder, onion powder, black pepper, cayenne pepper, orange juice, lime juice, lemon juice, soy sauce, olive oil, minced garlic and jalapeño and mix well. Place the steaks in the marinade, cover and refrigerate for at least 2 hours, and up to 10.

Preheat your Traeger grill to 450°F (232°C). Meanwhile, remove the steaks from the marinade and pat dry with paper towels. Discard the marinade.

Once the grill is preheated, cook the steaks for 4 to 5 minutes per side, rotating 90 degrees while cooking to create diamond grill marks. Remove the steaks from the grill when the internal temperature reaches 130°F (54°C) for medium rare. Transfer the steaks to a cutting board and allow them to rest, tented loosely in foil, for 10 minutes. Then slice and serve!

LAMB CHOPS WITH POMEGRANATE & FIG SALSA

COOK TIME
10 minutes (plus 5–10 minutes to rest)

YIELD
2 servings

PELLET
Any

TECHNIQUE
Hot & Fast (page 19)

EQUIPMENT
Silicone basting/pastry brush
Digital probe thermometer

INGREDIENTS
¼ cup (60 ml) pomegranate juice, chilled

½ tsp cornstarch

6 dried figs, diced

Arils from 1 whole pomegranate (about 1 cup [240 ml])

1 tsp fresh jalapeño, finely diced

1 tsp finely diced red onion

1 tsp finely chopped cilantro

Juice of ½ a lime

Splash of olive oil

Splash of balsamic vinegar (I used golden balsamic)

Kosher salt

Freshly ground black pepper

6 lamb loin chops (about 3 lbs [1.3 kg] total)

2 tbsp (26 g) herb-forward rub, such as Jacobsen's Steak Seasoning

Lamb that has been grilled on the Traeger is extra flavorful because you are cooking with real wood pellets. This recipe comes together very quickly, as you cook the lamb hot and fast on the Traeger. The salsa to accompany it blends some amazing autumnal flavors—definitely give it a try!

Preheat your Traeger grill to 450°F (232°C).

In a small saucepan, combine the cold pomegranate juice and cornstarch and whisk until blended. Cook on the stove over low heat, stirring constantly, until it reduces by half and makes a syrup. Remove from the heat and allow to cool completely.

In a medium bowl, combine the figs, pomegranate arils, jalapeño, onion, cilantro, lime juice, olive oil and vinegar and mix well. Add a few tablespoons (45 ml) of the pomegranate syrup to the salsa. Season with salt and pepper to taste and set aside.

Pat the lamb chops dry on both sides. Using a basting brush, coat each chop with the pomegranate syrup. Discard the leftover syrup. Season the chops with the rub and set aside.

Once the grill is preheated, cook the chops for about 5 minutes on each side. Remove the chops from the grill when the internal temperature reaches 130°F (54°C) for medium rare. Allow the chops to rest for 5 to 10 minutes, then serve with the pomegranate and fig salsa.

SMASH BURGERS

COOK TIME
10 minutes

YIELD
2 servings

PELLET
Any

TECHNIQUE
Hot & Fast (page 19)

EQUIPMENT
Cast-iron griddle or skillet

Flat spatula

Oven or grill mitt or
heat-proof gloves

INGREDIENTS
1 lb (454 g) ground beef

Cooking oil spray

¼ cup (52 g) rub, such as The
Gospel by Meat Church BBQ

4 slices American cheese

2 hamburger buns

Your favorite burger toppings
(I used pickle slices and a
quick homemade burger
sauce of equal parts
mayonnaise, ketchup and
chopped pickles)

This will quickly become your go-to method for cooking burgers for a tasty weeknight dinner. Be sure to use a cast-iron griddle or skillet, and let it get as hot as possible inside the grill to ensure the meat develops a great crust on the first side when you smash it. The crispy edges from this technique are so delicious. If you like, add some super thinly sliced white onions to the grill when you start your burgers, and smash them into the meat for an extra kick of flavor.

Preheat your Traeger grill to 400°F (204°C). Place a cast-iron griddle in the grill to heat up.

While the grill preheats, divide the ground beef into four equal parts and form them into loose balls.

Spray the griddle with cooking oil spray to prevent the meat from sticking. When the griddle is very hot, place the balls of ground beef, spaced about 2 inches (5 cm) apart from each other, on the griddle.

Using a flat spatula and oven mitt to protect your hand, smash the meat flat into thin patties (see the Fast Hack). Season each patty with the rub. After 2 minutes, flip the patties over and top each with a slice of cheese.

Place the buns onto an open section of the grill to warm them up. After 2 minutes, or when the cheese is melty, use the spatula to stack two patties onto a bottom bun.

Top with your favorite burger toppings and the top bun and enjoy.

FAST HACK! I have found that the best smashed burgers on the grill come with a little effort. Wear an oven or grill mitt or a pair of heat-proof gloves, and use the heel of your hand to press down on the spatula, as shown in the picture. I have a set of oven mitts dedicated to grilling!

THE ULTIMATE BBQ CHEESEBURGER

COOK TIME
15 minutes

YIELD
4 servings

PELLET
Any

TECHNIQUE
Hot & Fast (page 19)

EQUIPMENT
Cast-iron skillet or griddle

Small baking sheet (optional)

Burger press (optional, see the Fast Hack)

Digital temperature probe

INGREDIENTS
8 frozen store-bought onion rings

1 lb (454 g) ground beef

4 tbsp (52 g) seasoning, such as Holy Cow by Meat Church BBQ

4 slices pepper jack cheese

1 cup (225 g) pulled pork (leftovers from the Traditional Pulled Pork Shoulder recipe on page 94)

4 brioche buns

4 slices Bacon Candy (page 141, made ahead of time, see the Fast Hack)

½ cup (120 ml) BBQ sauce

Sometimes, there's nothing as delicious and indulgent as an amazing cheeseburger on a work night. I take my burgers to the next level by topping cheesy patties with candied bacon, onion rings, griddled leftover pulled pork and a generous dose of BBQ sauce. By using store-bought frozen onion rings, leftover Traditional Pulled Pork Shoulder (page 94) and Bacon Candy (page 141) that is made ahead of time, these burgers come together quickly, and you won't even miss the take-out container!

Preheat your Traeger grill to 450°F (232°C). Place a cast-iron skillet in the grill.

While the grill is preheating, cook the onion rings in the oven according to the package directions. You can also cook the onion rings in the grill on a small baking sheet placed next to the cast-iron skillet.

Using your hands or a burger press, form the ground beef into four patties about ¾ inch (2 cm) thick. Season the patties all over with the seasoning. Place the burgers in the hot cast-iron skillet, and cook for 4 minutes per side. For medium rare, cook them to an internal temperature of 145°F (63°C). Top each patty with a slice of cheese and allow it to melt. Transfer the burgers to a plate and tent them loosely with foil while you prepare the rest of the ingredients. Griddle the leftover pork in the cast-iron skillet for about 3 minutes until it is heated through and has crispy edges. Toast the buns in the grill until just golden.

Assemble the burgers by placing one patty on a toasted bottom bun. Top with a piece of candied bacon and two onion rings. Fill the onion rings with griddled pork and douse generously with BBQ sauce. Cap with the top bun and serve with a fork and knife.

FAST HACKS! I like to make the Bacon Candy ahead of time, or use leftovers. If you want to make it fresh with the burgers, follow the instructions on page 141 to prepare it before starting the burgers. Once it's ready, increase the temperature of the grill to 450°F (232°C) and place a cast-iron skillet or griddle inside to heat up.

If there's another tool you might want to add to your arsenal, I'd argue that a high-quality burger press is one to consider. By forming uniform, consistent patties, you will end up with finished burgers that are cooked evenly and predictably. Plus, it's a useful tool you can use in many burger recipes, including chicken and lamb.

BUFFALO CHICKEN BURGERS

COOK TIME
20 minutes

YIELD
4 servings

PELLET
Any

TECHNIQUE
Outdoor Oven (page 21)

EQUIPMENT
Digital temperature probe

INGREDIENTS
2 lbs (908 g) ground chicken

4 tsp (19 g) unsalted butter, divided (2 tsp melted)

½ cup (120 ml) hot sauce, such as Frank's, divided

1 tsp kosher salt

1 tsp freshly ground black pepper

2 celery ribs, thinly sliced on the diagonal

1 green onion, thinly sliced

¼ cup (32 g) crumbled blue cheese

¼ cup (60 ml) ranch salad dressing, plus more for serving

4 brioche buns

Chicken wings with a spicy buffalo sauce might be one of my most favorite foods. I've found a great way to make Smoke-Fried Wings on the grill (see page 55), and this recipe takes those classic buffalo flavors to a new level. The ground chicken patty is seasoned with buffalo sauce, and the flavors are locked in on the grill. The burger is topped with blue cheese and a celery slaw. It's buffalo wing night on a bun!

Preheat your Traeger grill to 350°F (177°C).

In a large bowl, combine the chicken, 2 teaspoons (10 ml) of melted butter and 1 tablespoon (15 ml) of the hot sauce. Using your hands, mix well. Season with the salt and pepper. Form the ground chicken into four even patties, then set aside.

In a small bowl, combine the celery, green onion, blue cheese and the ranch dressing in a bowl. Taste and adjust the seasoning as necessary. In a small saucepan, make the buffalo sauce by combining the remaining butter and hot sauce. Cook on the stove over low heat, keeping the sauce warm.

Once the grill is preheated, cook the chicken patties for about 10 minutes, flipping occasionally until the internal temperature reads 165°F (74°C). Toast the buns near the end of the cook for 2 minutes until golden.

Assemble the burgers with a spoonful of blue cheese and celery salad on each patty, a drizzle of buffalo sauce and additional ranch as desired.

STUFFED GREEK LAMB BURGERS

COOK TIME
10 minutes

YIELD
4 servings

PELLET
Any

TECHNIQUE
Hot & Fast (page 19)

EQUIPMENT
Cast-iron griddle or skillet
Burger press (optional)

A lamb burger is not something you can only get at a restaurant. These burgers are a Greek twist on the legendary "Juicy Lucy" burger that oozes with melted cheese when eaten. We like serving them in buns, but you could definitely use a pita pocket to go with your favorite Greek-inspired toppings like homemade tzatziki sauce, cucumber and tomato salad or olive tapenade.

Preheat your Traeger grill to 450°F (232°C). Place a cast-iron griddle in the grill to heat up.

In a small bowl, combine the feta cheese, cheddar cheese and oregano and set aside.

In a large bowl, combine the lamb, mint, parsley, lemon zest, garlic and olive oil. Using your hands or a burger press, form the lamb mixture into eight even, thin patties about ¼ inch (6 mm) thick.

INGREDIENTS

1 cup (115 g) crumbled feta cheese

½ cup (57 g) shredded sharp white cheddar cheese

2 tbsp (10 g) dried Greek oregano

1½ lbs (680 g) ground lamb

1 tbsp (14 g) chopped fresh mint

1 tbsp (14 g) chopped fresh parsley

Zest of 1 lemon

2 garlic cloves, minced

1 tbsp (15 ml) olive oil

Kosher salt, plus more for seasoning

Freshly ground black pepper

½ cup (60 ml) plain Greek yogurt

¼ cup (30 g) grated cucumber

Juice of ½ a lemon

Cooking oil

4 brioche buns

Toppings and sides of your choice, such as lettuce, tomatoes, red onions, cucumber and Kalamata olives

Assemble the stuffed burgers by placing 1 tablespoon (15 g) of the cheese mixture in the center of one of the prepared patties. Top with a second prepared patty. Press down firmly on the burger stack, and pinch around the edges to seal the two patties together. Return the stuffed patties to your burger press, if using, to make the shape and seal uniformly. Season both sides of the burger with salt and pepper. This makes one burger. Repeat with the other patties to make a total of four burgers. Set aside while you make the tzatziki sauce and allow the grill to finish preheating. You can also make the patties ahead of time and refrigerate them until ready to use.

To make the tzatziki sauce, in a small bowl, combine the yogurt, cucumber, lemon juice and a pinch of salt.

Lightly oil the preheated cast-iron griddle, and cook the burgers for 3 to 5 minutes per side until the internal temperature reaches 145°F (63°C). Transfer the burgers to a plate and tent loosely with foil. Lightly warm the buns in the grill while the burgers rest.

Assemble the burgers by topping each bun bottom with a dollop of tzatziki sauce, a patty, another dollop of sauce, lettuce and any other toppings you'd like. We like to serve these with a quick salad of tomatoes, red onions, chopped cucumber and a bunch of Kalamata olives.

FAST & DELICIOUS
CHICKEN & PORK

Chicken and pork are two BBQ standards, and the recipes in this chapter demonstrate both the variety and predictability of these protein categories. Rather than stop at the store to pick up a pre-roasted whole chicken, it's really simple to roast one at home in your Traeger. Once you get the technique down, the flavor options are limitless. The same goes for the other recipes in this chapter, which are all fast, efficient and affordable. Soon they'll be in your weekly rotation of delicious home-cooked weeknight dinners.

WHOLE TRAEGERED CHICKEN

COOK TIME
45 minutes (plus 15 minutes to sweat and 10 minutes to rest)

YIELD
4 servings

PELLET
Signature

TECHNIQUE
Outdoor Oven (page 21)

EQUIPMENT
Digital probe thermometer

INGREDIENTS
1 whole (5–7-lb [2.3–3-kg]) chicken

¼ cup (60 ml) olive oil

¼ cup (32 g) poultry rub, such as Traeger's Chicken Rub (see also the Classic Chicken Blend rub recipe on page 17)

Nothing beats Traeger chicken: juicy and full of flavor with a terrific hint of that Traeger smoke. This is one of the cooks I often recommend to people who are new to Traegering. Once you get the timing right, play with the flavors you use to season the chicken—your possibilities are endless! You'll never go back to a store-bought roasted chicken when you can throw one in your Traeger and get it to the table in just over an hour.

Preheat your Traeger grill to 450°F (232°C). Pat the chicken dry with paper towels, then apply an even coating of oil all over. Season liberally with the rub on all sides and allow it to sit for 15 minutes to sweat.

Place the whole chicken in the grill and cook for 45 minutes, until the internal temperature in the thickest part of the breast reaches 165°F (74°C). Allow it to rest for 10 minutes before carving or shredding.

FAST HACK! While this recipe is super simple, I encourage you to give it a try. You can serve the whole roasted chicken or use it in other recipes, such as Chicken Tinga Tacos (page 63) or a quick batch of enchiladas on the grill. You can even brush the chicken with your favorite BBQ sauce during the last ten minutes of cooking. Experiment with the flavor, and you'll have a different dinner every time!

FAST TIP: If you're looking to elevate dinner a bit, it's super fun to do a spin on the whole chicken and make grilled Cornish game hens instead—everyone gets their own bird! The recipe is easy to scale up or down to fit the size of your family or the number of dinner guests. I recommend spatchcocking these little birds—just snip out the backbone and press down with the palm of your hand to crack the breast bone. Then they will cook extremely quickly and evenly.

A great seasoning for Cornish game hens is a mix of equal parts garlic powder, onion powder, oregano, paprika, salt and pepper mixed with some olive oil to make a paste. Brush it on both sides of the birds and place them breast-side up on the grill. These should cook in about 25 to 30 minutes at 300°F (149°C).

SMOKED CHICKEN YAKITORI SKEWERS

COOK TIME
20–25 minutes (plus
15 minutes for marinating)

YIELD
4 servings

PELLET
Any

TECHNIQUE
Hot & Fast (page 19)

EQUIPMENT
Large bowl or shallow glass
baking dish with a cover (or
plastic wrap), for marinating

6 skewers (if bamboo or wood,
soak in warm water for
30 minutes)

Pastry brush

Digital probe thermometer

INGREDIENTS
½ cup (120 ml) soy sauce

¼ cup (60 ml) sake or mirin

2 tbsp (28 g) brown sugar

1 tbsp (8 g) grated fresh
ginger

1 garlic clove, minced

½ tsp sesame oil

1½ lbs (680 g) boneless,
skinless chicken thighs, cut
into 2-inch (5-cm) pieces

12 small shitake mushrooms

1 bunch green onions, cut
into 1½-inch (4-cm) pieces
(reserve some green onions
and slice thinly for garnish)

This is a great recipe for easy Japanese-style chicken on a stick. The chicken pieces are quickly marinated in a tasty sauce and then brushed with the same sauce as it cooks on a very hot Traeger. You could use smaller skewers to make appetizer-sized bites or serve full-sized skewers with rice and stir-fried vegetables.

In a large bowl or shallow glass baking dish, combine the soy sauce, sake, brown sugar, ginger, garlic and sesame oil. Reserve 4 tablespoons (60 ml) of the marinade and set aside. Add the chicken pieces to the marinade and stir to coat. Cover and allow the chicken to marinate for at least 15 minutes.

Preheat your Traeger grill to 400°F (204°C). Thread the chicken pieces, mushrooms and green onion pieces on skewers, alternating ingredients and leaving a little space between each piece. Discard the marinade.

Grill the skewers on the hot grill for 3 minutes, then brush with the reserved marinade. Turn the skewers and brush the other side with the marinade. Continue turning and basting for about 15 to 20 minutes, until the chicken is cooked through to an internal temperature of 165°F (74°C). Arrange the skewers on a platter, drizzle with the rest of the reserved marinade and sprinkle with the extra sliced green onions.

BBQ CHICKEN LOLLIPOPS

COOK TIME
55 minutes

YIELD
4-6 servings

PELLET
Pecan

TECHNIQUE
Outdoor Oven (page 21)

EQUIPMENT
Kitchen shears or sharp knife

Traeger chicken leg hanger (optional)

Digital probe thermometer

INGREDIENTS
12 chicken leg drumsticks

½ cup (64 g) poultry rub, such as Double Smoke by Spiceology

1 cup (240 ml) BBQ sauce, such as Head Country's Apple Habanero

These lollipopped chicken legs are delicious, easy to eat and fun to serve. With a little bit of prep, they cook evenly and are great for either a main course or an appetizer. You can ask your butcher to lollipop the drumsticks for you, which will make this recipe even easier to make, but if you have the time and the interest, it's worth giving it a try yourself. Served with baked potatoes and a green vegetable, these make a fun weeknight meal for your family.

Preheat your Traeger grill to 350°F (177°C). While the grill heats up, it's time to turn the drumsticks into lollipops!

Using a pair of kitchen shears or a sharp knife, remove the bottom part of the meat from the bone. Start by cutting just below the knuckle all the way around. Push the meat down to the other end, leaving the bone exposed. Trim to tidy up the meat, removing any tendons that may pop out.

Season the lollipops with your favorite poultry rub, and wrap the exposed part of the bones in foil to prevent them from burning and to give them a nice finished presentation. Place the drumsticks on the leg hanger, if using, or on the hot grill on their sides or standing on their ends, if possible. Pour the BBQ sauce into a large cup or bowl and keep nearby.

Cook the lollipops for about 35 minutes, until the internal temperature reaches 145°F (63°C). Remove the chicken from the grill, and dunk each drumstick, one at a time, in the BBQ sauce.

Increase the grill temperature to 400°F (204°C). Place the lollipops back in the grill and cook for about 20 minutes longer, until the internal temperature reaches 175°F (79°C). Remove the aluminum foil from the bones before serving.

SMOKE-FRIED WINGS

COOK TIME
1 hour (plus 15 minutes to sweat)

YIELD
2-3 servings

PELLET
Pecan

TECHNIQUE
Outdoor Oven (page 21)

EQUIPMENT
Dutch oven or deep cast-iron skillet for frying

Large slotted spoon

Small grill-proof saucepan or bowl

INGREDIENTS
2 lbs (908 g) chicken wings, both drums and flats

¼ cup (60 ml) olive oil

½ cup (64 g) poultry rub, such as The Blazin' Bird by Whiskey Bent BBQ

3 cups (720 ml) vegetable oil (or enough to fill a Dutch oven about 1 inch [2.5 cm] deep)

1 cup (240 ml) buffalo wing sauce (for an easy homemade version use 2 parts Frank's Red Hot Sauce and 1 part melted butter) or sauce of your choice

You have definitely had fried chicken wings. And you've likely had smoked wings. But when you have smoke-fried wings, you get the best of both. These come together in a little over an hour, but trust me—their smoky base flavor and crispy skin are worth the effort. Frying them in your grill keeps your kitchen clean, but I recommend getting the oil hot in the kitchen while the chicken smokes and then carefully transfering the pan of oil to your Traeger to save time. These are great finished with your favorite store-bought wing sauce, or use any of the BBQ sauce recipes offered on pages 158 to 161. If you want wings on the table in under an hour, increase the temperature of the grill to 275°F (135°C), which will cook the wings more quickly and only sacrifice a little of the smoked flavor.

Preheat your Traeger grill to 225°F (107°C), and turn on the Super Smoke feature if your grill has it.

In a large bowl, toss the chicken wings with olive oil until evenly coated. Sprinkle generously with the rub, being sure to cover all the sides thoroughly.

While the grill is heating up, let the chicken wings sit with the seasoning for about 15 minutes. This allows the flavors to start to work their way into the meat. Then cook them in the hot grill for about 45 minutes, until the internal temperature reaches 140°F (60°C).

Meanwhile, in a Dutch oven, heat the vegetable oil on the stove over medium-high heat until it reaches 350°F (177°C).

Remove the chicken from the grill, tent with foil and increase the grill temperature to 450°F (232°C). Very carefully transfer the Dutch oven with the hot oil to the Traeger. Pour the wing sauce in a grill-proof saucepan or bowl on the grill, and allow it to heat up while you fry the wings.

Fry the wings in the Dutch oven in small batches for 3 to 5 minutes, until the internal temperature reaches 175°F (79°C), which makes for a crispy skin and excellent bite. Remove them from the oil, drain briefly on paper towels and transfer the fried wings to a large bowl. Toss the wings with the warmed sauce. Serve with blue cheese dressing, ranch and your favorite veggies.

JUICY BONE-IN PORK CHOPS

COOK TIME
35–50 minutes (plus a few minutes to sweat and rest)

YIELD
4 servings

PELLET
Cherry

TECHNIQUE
Reverse Sear (page 19)

EQUIPMENT
Digital probe thermometer

INGREDIENTS
3 tbsp (42 g) brown sugar

2 tbsp (28 g) kosher salt

2 tbsp (14 g) freshly ground black pepper

1 tsp smoked paprika

1 tsp ground mustard

1 tsp garlic powder

1 tsp chili powder

¼ tsp cinnamon

4 bone-in, thick-cut pork chops

Reverse searing a bone-in pork chop results in a juicy, tender and delicious quick dinner. These are not the dry, bland pork chops of old! I like the presentation of a bone-in pork chop—and the resulting rib bites you get once you cut into your meat—but you can make this recipe with boneless pork chops. A bone-in cut also stays a bit juicier during the cook because the bone insulates the edge of the meat and prevents moisture from escaping. As with all reverse sears in this book, the actual cook time is dependent on the thickness of your cut, but the process remains the same. And it is absolutely worth it to cook your pork chops with this technique, because you will end up with jucy, tender pork that has a nice smoke flavor.

If time is of the essence, bump up the grill temperature to 250°F (121°C) or 275°F (135°C), which will speed up the cook, though the pork will be a little less smoky. The rub I recommend making for this recipe includes savory spices, brown sugar and a tiny bit of cinnamon, but you can use another seasoning of your choice, if you prefer. Serve with a homemade BBQ sauce from pages 158 to 161.

Preheat your Traeger grill to 225°F (107°C), and turn on the Super Smoke feature if your grill has it.

In a small bowl, combine the brown sugar, salt, pepper, smoked paprika, ground mustard, garlic powder, chili powder and cinnamon and mix well. Season the pork chops on all sides with the rub. Allow the meat to sweat for a few minutes, then place the chops in the center of the hot grill.

Cook the pork chops for about 30 to 45 minutes, checking the internal temperature after 20 minutes with a digital probe thermometer. When the internal temperature reaches 110°F (43°C), transfer the pork chops to a cutting board and tent them with foil. Increase the grill temperature to 450°F (232°C) and allow it to heat up for 8 to 10 minutes with the lid closed.

Return the pork chops to the hot grill and sear each side for about 90 seconds, turning 45 degrees halfway through to create diamond grill marks. Perfect pork should be cooked to an internal temperature of 145°F (63°C), so remove the chops from the grill when the temperature reaches 140°F (60°C), to account for the carryover cooking. Transfer the pork chops back to the cutting board to briefly rest before serving.

ORANGE, CHIPOTLE & BOURBON GLAZED PORK TENDERLOINS

COOK TIME
40 minutes (plus 10 minutes to sweat and 5 minutes to rest)

YIELD
4 servings

PELLET
Pecan

TECHNIQUE
Reverse Sear (page 19)

EQUIPMENT
Cast-iron skillet, griddle or GrillGrates
Pastry brush
Blender or food processor
Small grill-proof saucepan
Digital probe thermometer

INGREDIENTS
1 (1½-lb [680-g]) pork tenderloin, trimmed
2 tbsp (30 ml) bourbon whiskey, divided
2 tbsp (29 g) pork rub, such as Double Smoke by Spiceology
2 garlic cloves
Juice of 1 navel orange
Juice of ½ a lime
1 tbsp (15 ml) hot honey (or substitute equal parts honey and chili flakes)
3 canned chipotle peppers in adobo sauce
1 tsp olive oil
¼ tsp cumin
¼ tsp freshly ground black pepper
¼ tsp achiote powder (see Fast Hack)
¼ tsp garlic powder
1 tsp kosher salt

This easy pork tenderloin is reverse seared, producing a perfectly cooked, juicy result every time. It's important to note that pork should be cooked to an internal temperature of 145°F (63°C), which will yield a tender, moist bite that's safe to eat. The glaze is spicy—combining both hot honey and chipotle peppers. If you're not a fan of spice, just use fewer peppers or substitute ketchup instead and use regular honey. If you need to speed up the cook even more, you could increase the initial temperature of the grill to 250°F (121°C) or 275°F (135°C), but the flavor will be a bit less smoky.

Preheat your Traeger grill to 225°F (107°C), and turn on the Super Smoke feature if your grill has it. Place GrillGrates or a cast-iron skillet in the grill to heat up.

Season the pork tenderloin by first brushing it lightly in ½ teaspoon or so of bourbon whiskey on all sides with a pastry brush and then season it liberally with the rub. Allow the meat to sweat for about 10 minutes after seasoning.

While the pork is resting, in a blender, combine the garlic, orange and lime juices, honey, chipotle peppers, olive oil, cumin, black pepper, achiote powder, garlic powder, salt and the remaining bourbon whiskey. Blend until well combined and smooth. Transfer the sauce to a small grill-proof saucepan and place the saucepan in the grill.

Cook the pork tenderloin in the grill for about 35 minutes, until the internal temperature reaches 130°F (54°C). Twice during the cook, brush the tenderloin with the chipotle sauce that has been warming in the grill.

When the internal temperature reaches 130°F (54°C), transfer the tenderloin to a cutting board and tent it loosely with foil. Increase the temperature of your grill to 450°F (232°C). Once the grill reaches 450°F (232°C), sear the pork on the hot GrillGrates for 90 seconds per side, rotating 45 degrees halfway through to create diamond grill marks. If using a cast-iron skillet, sear all over for about 3 minutes total for a great crust. Remove the tenderloin from the grill when the internal temperature reaches 140°F (60°C).

Allow the meat to rest for 5 minutes, then slice it into medallions and enjoy.

FAST HACK! Achiote is a powder made of annatto seeds, which impart a slightly tart flavor and bright red color to recipes like this one. You can often find it in the Hispanic foods aisle of your grocery store. You can absolutely omit it from this recipe if you're not able to find it.

GRILLED PORK SHOULDER STEAKS WITH HERB GREMOLATA

COOK TIME
10 minutes (plus
15 minutes to sweat
and 10 minutes to rest)

YIELD
4 servings

PELLET
Cherry

TECHNIQUE
Hot & Fast (page 19)

EQUIPMENT
Digital probe thermometer

PORK STEAKS
1 tbsp (6 g) ground cumin

1 tbsp (7 g) ground mustard

2 tsp (8 g) brown sugar

1 tsp freshly ground black pepper

1 tsp garlic powder

1 tsp onion powder

2 tsp (8 g) kosher salt

4 (¾-inch [2-cm]-thick) pork shoulder steaks

GREMOLATA
¼ cup (32 g) finely chopped parsley

3 tbsp (43 g) lemon zest

2 garlic cloves, minced

1 tbsp (4 g) finely chopped rosemary

1 tbsp (4 g) finely chopped thyme

1 tbsp (4 g) finely chopped basil

2 tsp (10 ml) olive oil

Kosher salt

Freshly ground black pepper

Before my wife and I made our first trip to Austin, Texas, we had never had pork shoulder steaks. Snow's BBQ in the Texas Hill Country is famous for all their BBQ, but their pork steaks are incredible and unexpected. They are slow cooked in their famous pits and have a strong traditional BBQ flavor. This is my unique take on them, seasoned with a blend of warm spices and cooked over high heat until they hit the perfect pork temperature of 145°F (63°C). Served with a gremolata of fresh herbs and lemon zest, this is not your usual BBQ cook. But give it a try!

To make the pork rub, in a small bowl, combine the cumin, ground mustard, brown sugar, pepper, garlic powder, onion powder and salt and mix well. Season the pork steaks generously on both sides with the rub, and allow them to sweat for 15 minutes.

Meanwhile, preheat your Traeger grill to 450°F (232°C). Make the gremolata while the grill heats up. In the same small bowl that you used to prepare the rub, combine the parsley, lemon zest, garlic, rosemary, thyme, basil and olive oil and stir to combine. Season with salt and pepper to taste and set aside.

Cook the seasoned pork steaks on the hot grill for about 3 minutes per side, until the internal temperature reaches 140°F (60°C).

Transfer the pork steaks to a cutting board, and allow it to rest, tented loosely with foil, for 10 minutes. When ready to serve, slice the steaks thinly and spoon the gremolata over the top.

COOK TIME
1 hour, 10 minutes if cooking a fresh chicken; 23 minutes if using leftover chicken

YIELD
4 servings

PELLET
Signature

TECHNIQUE
Outdoor Oven (page 21)

EQUIPMENT
Cast-iron skillet

Blender

Digital probe thermometer

Oven or grill mitts or heat-proof gloves

TINGA SAUCE
1 tbsp (15 ml) vegetable oil

1 cup (150 g) chopped yellow onion

2 garlic cloves, minced

2–3 chipotle peppers in adobo sauce, roughly chopped

1 tbsp (5 g) dried oregano

1 tbsp (6 g) ground cumin

1 (14.5-oz [411-g]) can fire-roasted tomatoes, with liquid

½ cup (120 ml) chicken broth

CHICKEN TINGA TACOS

SMOKED CHICKEN

1 whole chicken, spatchcocked (or shredded cooked chicken leftover from the Whole Traegered Chicken recipe on page 48)

3 tbsp (28 g) rub, such as Bada Bing Dry Brine by Spiceology

CILANTRO-JALAPEÑO CREMA

½ cup (120 ml) Mexican crema or sour cream thinned with milk

Large handful fresh cilantro

Juice of 1 lime

½ a fresh jalapeño, roughly chopped

Kosher salt

Freshly ground black pepper

TACO ASSEMBLY

Fresh flour tortillas

Crumbled cotija cheese

Chopped tomatoes

Sliced red onions

Cubed avocado

This is a delicious recipe to make for Taco Tuesday. The sauce is spicy and strongly flavored, and it complements the simplicity of the pulled chicken really well. Top with your favorite taco toppings and enjoy. To make it super easy, we love to use leftover Whole Traegered Chicken (page 48) to make the tacos. You can cook the chicken the night you make the tacos, or use leftover chicken from the night before!

Preheat your Traeger grill to 400°F (204°C). Place a cast-iron skillet in the grill.

Prepare the tinga sauce by heating the vegetable oil in the hot skillet on the grill, then add the onion and garlic and sauté for about 10 minutes, until translucent. Stir in the chipotle peppers, oregano, and cumin, and cook for 3 minutes until well combined. Stir in the tomatoes and chicken broth. Simmer for 10 minutes until the liquid reduces a bit.

Carefully transfer the sauce ingredients to a blender, and blend until nearly smooth. Return the sauce to the cast-iron skillet and set aside. The sauce can be made ahead of time and refrigerated until ready to use. (If not making ahead of time, rinse and dry the blender to use it for making the crema while the chicken is roasting.)

Keep the grill heated to 400°F (204°C) to roast the chicken.

Pat the chicken dry with paper towels and season it generously with the rub. I used a Grill Dads dry brine by Spiceology, which is a great all-around chicken rub. Place the whole seasoned chicken on the grate of the grill. Cook for about 45 minutes, until the internal temperature reaches 165°F (74°C) and the skin is crispy.

Prepare the cilantro-jalapeño crema while the chicken is cooking. In a blender, combine the crema, cilantro, lime juice and jalapeño and blend until smooth. Season with salt and pepper to taste and refrigerate.

Remove the cooked chicken from the grill and allow it to cool slightly. Using gloves, remove the skin and shred the meat.

When you're ready to build the tacos, gently heat the tinga sauce in a grill-proof pan or in a saucepan on the stove until warm throughout and fold in the pulled chicken. Warm the tortillas and pile them with chicken and sauce, crumbled cotija cheese, chopped tomatoes, sliced red onions, cubes of avocado and a dollop of cilantro-jalapeño crema and enjoy.

FAST HACK! I love cotija cheese on my tacos. You can usually find it in the cheese aisle of your grocery store. It's often sold in a round block. It's crumbly and salty—somewhere between feta and Parmesan—with a texture similar to strained ricotta cheese. It's great on all Mexican food, especially grilled corn and nachos! You can use cheddar cheese if you prefer or have a hard time finding cotija.

"BREAKFAST FOR DINNER" TRAEGER CASSEROLE

COOK TIME
40 minutes

YIELD
4–6 servings

PELLET
Any

TECHNIQUE
Outdoor Oven (page 21)

EQUIPMENT
Grill-proof ceramic or glass baking dish

INGREDIENTS
1 tbsp (14 g) unsalted butter

½ lb (227 g) frozen shredded hash brown potatoes, uncooked

1 lb (454 g) ground breakfast sausage, cooked and drained

6 large eggs

1 cup (240 ml) milk

1 tsp kosher salt

1 tsp freshly ground black pepper

Dash of hot sauce

1 cup (113 g) shredded cheddar cheese, divided

What is a cookbook without at least one casserole recipe? For us, breakfast for dinner is a great weeknight solution, and when it's cooked on the Traeger, it's even more delicious and unexpected. This recipe can be made ahead of time and refrigerated until you're ready to cook. We often assemble it the night before and put it in the fridge until the following evening. While the grill heats up, we prep some fresh fruit to accompany it. It's the best of breakfast all in one dish—eggs, potatoes, sausage and cheese. See the Fast Hack below for some ideas on mixing up the flavors.

Preheat your Traeger grill to 450°F (232°C), and allow it to heat up for 15 minutes with the lid closed.

Grease the sides and bottom of a baking dish with the butter. Spread the potatoes in an even layer at the bottom of the dish. Top with the breakfast sausage. In a large bowl, whisk together the eggs, milk, salt, pepper and hot sauce until well combined, then stir in half of the cheese.

Pour the egg mixture over the potatoes and sausage, and use a fork to poke vertically into the dish, allowing the egg to seep down to the potato layer. This can be made ahead of time and kept in the fridge until you are ready to cook.

Place the baking dish in the hot grill and bake for 25 minutes. Sprinkle with the remaining cheese, and continue cooking for another 15 minutes, until the egg is set and the top is golden brown. Allow to cool slightly and serve.

FAST HACK! We use the eggs, potatoes and cheese as the common base for this recipe and often add a layer of leftover pulled pork or chopped up brisket or ham in place of the sausage. You can also add canned green chiles for a spicy kick.

SMOKE-ROASTED CHICKEN WITH LEMONS

COOK TIME
45 minutes

YIELD
4 servings

PELLET
Pecan or cherry

TECHNIQUE
Outdoor Oven (page 21)

EQUIPMENT
Grill-proof baking dish
Digital probe thermometer

INGREDIENTS
2 lbs (908 g) bone-in, skin-on whole chicken legs

3 tbsp (43 g) all-purpose or poultry seasoning, such as Garlic Junky by Spiceology or the Classic Chicken Blend rub recipe on page 17

2 tsp (12 g) kosher salt

2 tsp (6 g) freshly ground black pepper

1 lemon, sliced into thin rounds

1 red Fresno pepper, quartered lengthwise

1 small bunch fresh thyme

2 heads garlic, cut in half

½ cup (120 ml) olive oil

Crusty French bread, for serving

This recipe is adapted from a favorite that we used to cook in the oven. By cooking in your Traeger grill, you keep your kitchen cool and clean, and your chicken comes out juicy, flavorful and delicious. In just about an hour, you can serve a delicious, unique take on roasted chicken. It is best served with crusty French bread for soaking up the juices.

Preheat your Traeger grill to 400°F (204°C). Arrange the chicken legs in a grill-proof baking dish. Season the chicken liberally on all sides with the rub, salt and pepper.

Place the lemon slices, Fresno pepper, thyme and garlic heads in the dish with the chicken. Drizzle the olive oil over all the ingredients, mix gently to combine and rearrange all the ingredients so they are in a single layer in the dish. Make sure the garlic halves are cut side down in the oil.

Roast the chicken for about 45 minutes, until the internal temperature reaches 165°F (74°C). Transfer the chicken to a serving platter, and drizzle the pan juices on top.

Serve with warm, crusty French bread for dipping. The melty roasted garlic cloves are especially delicious spread on the bread.

GREEN CHILE CHICKEN CORDON BLEU

This is not your grandma's chicken cordon bleu. Grilling the chicken instead of frying it gives this classic dish a tasty twist, and the green chiles add a bit of southwestern pop. You can roast your own green chiles on the grill or buy them pre-roasted. However, the little extra effort it takes to do them yourself pays off. We assemble this dish the night before, wrapping the chicken tightly in plastic wrap, and refrigerate it until the grill is hot. Dinner in under an hour!

COOK TIME
35 minutes if using pre-roasted chiles; 55 minutes if roasting your own (plus 5 minutes to rest)

YIELD
4 servings

PELLET
Signature

TECHNIQUE
Outdoor Oven (page 21)

EQUIPMENT
Tongs
Wax paper or plastic wrap
Meat mallet
Small grill-proof baking sheet or baking dish
Digital probe thermometer

INGREDIENTS
4 whole fresh or canned Anaheim or Hatch green chiles

1 tbsp (15 ml) vegetable oil

4 boneless, skinless chicken breasts (get the largest ones you can find, about 6 oz [170 g] each)

2 tsp (12 g) kosher salt

2 tsp (6 g) freshly ground black pepper

8 slices Swiss cheese

8 slices deli ham

4 tbsp (58 g) soft cheese, such as Boursin

4 slices uncooked bacon

¼ cup (46 g) Spicy Bloody Mary seasoning by Spiceology

If you're roasting fresh chilies, preheat your Traeger grill to 400°F (204°C). Rub the outside of each chile with vegetable oil. Place the chiles in the grill as it heats up, and allow them to cook for 10 minutes. The skins should start to turn dark and blister. Rotate the peppers with a pair of tongs and continue to cook for another 10 minutes. Transfer the roasted peppers to a metal bowl and seal the bowl tightly with plastic wrap. Allow the peppers to steam for at least 15 minutes while you prepare the chicken.

Reduce the temperature of your grill to 350°F (177°C). If you used pre-roasted chiles, preheat the grill to this temperature.

Butterfly the chicken breasts and then pound the meat to ¼ inch (6 mm) thickness, placing each one between two pieces of wax paper or plastic wrap. Be careful not to rip a hole in the chicken. Repeat with each chicken breast and set them aside.

Peel the roasted peppers by running them under a stream of cold water, and carefully remove the charred skin. Slice the peppers open to flatten them and remove the seeds, if desired.

Place one pounded chicken breast on a cutting board, cut side up. Season with salt and pepper. Lay 2 slices of Swiss cheese atop the chicken, then 2 slices of ham atop the cheese. Spread 1 tablespoon (15 g) of soft cheese on the ham and top with 1 green chile. Roll up the chicken to make a roulade, then secure it with 1 slice of bacon. Place the chicken breast on a baking sheet with the bacon seam down. Season the outside of the chicken liberally with the seasoning. Repeat with the remaining chicken breasts.

Place the baking sheet with the chicken in the hot grill and cook for 30 to 35 minutes, until the internal temperature in the thickest part of the chicken roulades reads 165°F (74°C). Remove them from the grill and allow them to rest for 5 minutes before slicing.

LIGHTNING FAST
FISH &
SEAFOOD

Fish and seafood are one of the quickest things you can cook on the grill, which makes them great protein options to mix up your weeknight dinners. The wood-fired flavor imparted by cooking on the Traeger is an added bonus. For the fish recipes, you can substitute your favorite fish or whatever you have on hand. Likewise, the clams in the Clams in Spicy Red Broth recipe (page 76) can be swapped for mussels. In many cases, having a good cast-iron skillet for cooking seafood will make your life easier. Experiment with swapping out different ingredients to switch up the flavors for interesting, tasty dinners any night of the week.

THAI HALIBUT EN PAPILLOTE

COOK TIME
20 minutes

YIELD
2 servings

PELLET
Hickory, maple, cherry or a blend

TECHNIQUE
Outdoor Oven (page 21)

EQUIPMENT
Pink butcher paper or parchment paper
Baking sheet
Digital probe thermometer

COMPOUND BUTTER
4 tbsp (56 g) unsalted butter, softened
2 tbsp (32 g) Thai red curry paste
1 tsp Thai curry seasoning
2 garlic cloves, minced

HALIBUT PACKETS
10 oz (283 g) portabella mushrooms, thinly sliced
2 (6-oz [170-g]) halibut fillets
Kosher salt
Freshly ground black pepper
1 serrano pepper, thinly sliced
¼ cup (12 g) chopped scallions
2 tbsp (2 g) thinly julienned basil
2 tbsp (2 g) cilantro leaves
Cooked sticky white rice, for serving

Cooking *en papillote*, or in a paper or parchment packet, often happens in an oven, but we've adapted this recipe to work perfectly in the Traeger. Fish cooked en papillote emerges as moist, flaky and flavorful. This recipe is simple and fast, as all the components of each serving are tucked into a packet and cooked together. You can adapt the contents of each packet to the picky eaters in your house, and cleanup is pretty simple with very little prep. Once cooked, the packets go from the grill to the plate and make for a dramatic presentation. We serve this dish with sticky white rice and some veggies for an easy and delicious post-work meal.

Preheat your Traeger grill to 400°F (204°C) and allow it to heat up for 15 minutes with the lid closed.

While the grill preheats, prepare the compound butter by combining the softened butter, curry paste, curry seasoning and garlic. Mix until smooth and well-incorporated. Place the butter mixture on a square of plastic wrap, roll it tightly into a log and refrigerate for 10 to 15 minutes while preparing the other ingredients.

Cut two 18-inch (45-cm) squares of butcher paper or parchment paper. Place one square at the center of your work surface. Place half of the mushroom slices in the center of each piece of paper. Top each portion of mushrooms with a halibut fillet and season lightly with salt and pepper. Top the halibut pieces with half of the serrano slices, scallions, basil and cilantro. Cut the prepared compound butter into quarters and place two pieces on top of each piece of halibut.

Bring the top and bottom of the butcher paper together and fold to seal. Bring in the sides of the paper and fold to create a tightly sealed packet. Place the prepared packets on a baking sheet, then place the baking sheet in the preheated grill to cook for 20 minutes. Use a digital probe thermometer to check the internal temperature of the fish after 20 minutes, and remove the packets from the grill when the internal temperature reaches 145°F (63°C).

Place each packet on a dinner plate with a serving of sticky white rice.

GRILLED SALMON WITH SPINACH PESTO

COOK TIME
25 minutes

YIELD
4 servings

PELLET
Signature

TECHNIQUE
Outdoor Oven (page 21)

EQUIPMENT
Pink butcher paper or parchment paper

Pastry brush

Digital probe thermometer

INGREDIENTS
1 tbsp (14 g) unsalted butter, melted

Juice of ½ a lemon

½ a lemon, cut into thin slices

1 (1–1½-lb [454–680-g]) salmon fillet

4 tbsp (46 g) Spicy Bloody Mary seasoning by Spiceology

Spinach Pesto (page 166), for serving

At least once a week, we like to throw a piece of salmon on the grill for a quick, healthy and easy dinner. You can season it with whatever flavor profile you prefer, but this recipe calls for salmon that has been simply seasoned with Spiceology's Spicy Bloody Mary seasoning. We cook our salmon to about medium—135°F (57°C)—which keeps the fish tender and moist. Spinach Pesto (page 166) goes great with this dish.

Preheat your Traeger grill to 375°F (191°C). While it's heating up, in a small bowl, stir together the butter and lemon juice and set aside.

On a piece of pink butcher paper or parchment paper, arrange the lemon slices in a single layer. Place the salmon fillet on top of the lemon slices, skin side down. With a pastry brush, brush the entire surface of the fish with the butter-lemon mixture, then coat the fish generously with the seasoning.

Put the parchment paper with the fish directly on the grates of the hot grill, and cook for about 25 minutes. Begin checking the internal temperature of the fish after about 15 minutes. Remove the salmon from the grill when the internal temperature reaches 135°F (57°C).

Cut the fish into four portions and serve with Spinach Pesto on the side.

FAST HACK! I like to cook fish like salmon on a piece of parchment or butcher paper in the grill, as it makes the grill less messy and prevents the fish from falling through the grates. By placing the lemons between the paper and the skin, the fish skin is less likely to stick to the paper.

CLAMS IN SPICY RED BROTH

COOK TIME
15–20 minutes

YIELD
2 servings

PELLET
Any

TECHNIQUE
Hot & Fast (page 19)

EQUIPMENT
Cast-iron skillet or Dutch oven
with a grill-proof lid

INGREDIENTS
¼ cup (60 ml) olive oil

2 small shallots, sliced

1 garlic clove, minced

1 Fresno pepper, thinly sliced

3 tbsp (48 g) tomato paste

2 cups (300 g) whole cherry
tomatoes

2 tbsp (30 g) Garlic Junky
seasoning by Spiceology

1 cup (240 ml) white wine

2 lbs (908 g) clams, scrubbed

6 tbsp (84 g) unsalted butter,
cubed

2 tbsp (6 g) chopped chives

Crusty bread, for serving

1 lemon, cut into wedges

This is an unexpectedly delicious meal to cook on the grill. You don't often find recipes for cooking clams in a smoker, but if you like shellfish, you definitely need to try it! This dish comes together very quickly, and the spicy, smoky broth that results from the clams letting off their juices is just delicious. Be sure to serve with crunchy bread to mop up the sauce. You could use this same technique with other shellfish, such as mussels, with either the same ingredients or variations on the flavors.

Preheat your Traeger grill to 450°F (232°C). Place a cast-iron skillet or Dutch oven in the grill to heat up. Add the olive oil to the skillet and allow it to get hot.

Add the shallots, garlic and Fresno pepper to the skillet, and cook until just softened, stirring frequently. Stir in the tomato paste and mix well. Add the cherry tomatoes and Garlic Junky seasoning, and stir for about 5 minutes, until the tomatoes start to burst. Pour in the white wine and stir. Cook for 3 additional minutes until the liquid has reduced a bit.

Add the clams and butter to the skillet and stir to combine. Cover the skillet and allow to cook for 8 to 10 minutes, until the clams have opened. Throw away any clams that haven't opened naturally.

Transfer everything to a serving bowl, garnish with the chives and serve with crusty bread and lemon wedges.

FAST HACK! It's important to clean your clams very well before cooking them. When you get home from work, put the clams in a bowl of cold water with a generous scoop of kosher salt. As the clams breathe, they'll expel the grit inside their shells, making for a better cook.

SMOKED OYSTERS

COOK TIME
8–10 minutes

YIELD
4 servings

PELLET
Signature

TECHNIQUE
Hot & Fast (page 19)

EQUIPMENT
Small grill-proof bowl or saucepan

INGREDIENTS
12 whole fresh oysters
2 tbsp (28 g) salted butter
2 tbsp (30 ml) hot sauce

While raw oysters are delicious, oysters that have been quickly cooked on a smoky Traeger are particularly special. This recipe comes together in no time and is great as an appetizer or a main, especially if you are in the mood for a surf-and-turf dinner.

Preheat your Traeger grill to 400°F (204°C).

Place the oysters directly on the hot grill and cook for 8 to 10 minutes, until they start to open up.

While the oysters are cooking, place the butter in a small grill-proof bowl or saucepan in the Traeger to melt.

Remove the oysters from the grill and pop open the shells. They should open easily. If any oysters don't open easily, discard them. Spoon some of the butter over the oysters and top with a dash of hot sauce.

BUTTER-BASTED SMOKED LOBSTER TAILS

COOK TIME
20 minutes

YIELD
2 servings

PELLET
Any

TECHNIQUE
Outdoor Oven (page 21)

EQUIPMENT
Kitchen shears
Pastry brush
Digital probe thermometer

INGREDIENTS
2 whole lobster tails, shell on

4 tbsp (56 g) unsalted butter, melted

2 tbsp (26 g) seafood rub, such as Garlic Junky seasoning by Spiceology

2 lemons, cut in half

You could make these lobster tails as a stand-alone main for a great meal, or pair them with a Traeger-grilled steak for an amazing surf-and-turf combo. By cutting the lobster meat out of the shell and placing it on top, you maintain the shape of the tail and have a dramatic presentation that's easy to eat and cooks very quickly. As you cook the lobster, put some lemon halves cut side down on the grill and serve this simple dish with caramelized lemon wedges. An amazing and decadent weeknight meal!

Preheat your Traeger grill to 375°F (191°C).

Using kitchen shears, cut down the middle of each lobster tail shell, starting at the open side and stopping just short of the fan. Carefully pull the lobster meat out of the shell and place it on top of the shell. The meat will remain connected to the shell closest to the fan.

With a pastry brush, coat the lobster meat with melted butter and season with the rub. Place the tails in the preheated grill and cook for 20 minutes, or until the internal temperature reaches 135°F (57°C). Brush the lobster tails twice while they cook with the remaining butter. Also while the lobster cooks, place the lemon halves cut side down on the grill to caramelize a bit. Grill for about 5 minutes, then set aside.

When the lobster tails reach 135°F (57°C), transfer them to plates. Serve with the grilled lemon halves and enjoy.

FAST HACK! Another way to add flavor to a perfectly cooked lobster tail is to mix up the butter you use. Check out the compound butter recipes on page 162 for a selection of unique flavors to try. You can skip the refrigeration step in the process, as you'll want the butter melted in this application anyway!

COOK TIME
20 minutes

YIELD
6 tacos (3 servings)

PELLET
Signature

TECHNIQUE
Hot & Fast (page 19)

EQUIPMENT
For beer-battered fish: Cast-iron skillet or Dutch oven

For baked fish: Pink butcher paper or parchment paper

Digital probe thermometer

CITRUS SLAW
¼ head green cabbage, chopped into small pieces

2 tbsp (29 g) thinly sliced red onion

2 tbsp (29 g) thinly sliced orange (or yellow or red) bell pepper

1 tbsp (14 g) diced jalapeño

Juice of ½ a lime

1 tsp olive oil

½ tsp kosher salt, plus more to taste

½ tsp garlic powder

½ tsp cumin

¼ tsp honey

Freshly ground black pepper

BAJA FISH TACOS

BAJA CREMA

¼ cup (60 ml) sour cream

¼ cup (60 ml) mayonnaise

Juice of ½ a lime

2 tbsp (16 g) chili powder

2 tbsp (12 g) cumin

1 tbsp (10 g) garlic powder

1 tbsp (7 g) onion powder

1 tbsp (5 g) cayenne pepper

Kosher salt

Freshly ground black pepper

BEER-BATTERED BAJA FISH

Vegetable oil for frying

1 cup (125 g) flour

2 tbsp (16 g) chili powder

2 tbsp (12 g) cumin

1 tbsp (10 g) garlic powder

1 tbsp (7 g) onion powder

1 tbsp (5 g) cayenne pepper

1 cup (240 ml) Mexican-style beer

Juice of 1 lime

1 lb (454 g) skinless cod, cut into 1-inch (2.5-cm)-wide strips

Kosher salt

OR GRILLED BAJA FISH

Juice of 1 lime

2 tbsp (30 ml) mayonnaise

2 tbsp (16 g) chili powder

2 tbsp (12 g) cumin

1 tbsp (10 g) garlic powder

1 tbsp (7 g) onion powder

1 tbsp (5 g) cayenne pepper

1 lb (454 g) skinless cod, cut into 3-inch (8-cm)-wide strips

TO SERVE

Fresh tortillas

Lime wedges

Fresh cilantro (optional)

Fresh fish tacos are both light and filling. This recipe uses a blend of seasonings to create a very flavorful beer batter that pairs nicely with delicately cooked cod and citrus slaw. Traditional fish tacos are beer-battered and fried, but you can simplify the recipe by grilling the fish in your Traeger. Both variations are outlined below. I particularly like making the fried version on the grill, as it limits the oil splatter and fried smell in the house. A Traeger is the perfect vessel to cook fried food in!

To make the slaw, in a medium bowl, combine the cabbage, onion, bell pepper, jalapeño, lime juice, olive oil, salt, garlic powder, cumin and honey and mix well. Season with salt and pepper to taste and set aside.

To make the crema, in a small bowl, combine the sour cream, mayonnaise, lime juice, chili powder, cumin, garlic powder, onion powder and cayenne pepper and mix well. Season with salt and pepper to taste and set aside.

The slaw and the crema can be made ahead and refrigerated for up to 3 hours, if preferred.

To make the beer-battered fish, preheat your Traeger grill to 450°F (232°C). Place a cast-iron skillet or Dutch oven on the stove with about ¾ inch (2 cm) of vegetable oil to heat up while you prepare the other ingredients.

In a small bowl, combine the flour, chili powder, cumin, garlic powder, onion powder and cayenne pepper. Slowly whisk in the beer and lime juice until the batter is smooth with no lumps. Check the oil temperature, and when it hits 350°F (177°C), you are ready to fry. Dip the fish pieces in batter, and fry them in batches until they are golden brown and cooked through, about 2 minutes per side. Carefully remove the fish from the oil and drain on paper towels. Season each piece lightly with salt and cook the remaining fish the same way.

To make the grilled fish, preheat your Traeger grill to 400°F (204°C). In a small bowl, combine the lime juice, mayonnaise, chili powder, cumin, garlic powder, onion powder and cayenne pepper. On a square of pink butcher paper or parchment paper, place the cod portions and spoon the mayonnaise mixture on top. Cook the fish on the paper in the hot grill for about 15 minutes, until the fish's internal temperature reaches 140°F (60°C). Remove the fish from the grill and break into big flakes with a fork.

Assemble the tacos by lightly toasting and heating the tortillas on the grill, then smear each with 1 tablespoon (15 ml) of crema. Top with a handful of slaw and a few pieces of fish. Serve with a squeeze of lime and cilantro leaves, if desired.

GARLIC JUNKY SMOKED SHRIMP SCAMPI

COOK TIME
20 minutes

YIELD
4 servings

PELLET
Any

TECHNIQUE
Reverse Sear (page 19)

EQUIPMENT
Cast-iron skillet

INGREDIENTS

8 oz (227 g) dry fettuccine pasta

1 lb (454 g) raw jumbo shrimp, peeled and deveined

1 tsp olive oil

4 tsp (12 g) Garlic Junky seasoning by Spiceology, divided (see Fast Hack)

¼ cup (60 ml) dry white wine

6 tbsp (84 g) butter

Juice of 1 lemon

½ tsp red pepper flakes

2 tsp (3 g) chopped fresh parsley

Kosher salt

Freshly ground black pepper

When we created my line of rubs with Spiceology, I knew I wanted something that would be an all-purpose, garlicky staple. Little did we expect it would turn out as delicious as it did and become so popular. It is great to use with a variety of proteins and cooks, but using it as the base for shrimp scampi is especially delicious. Soaking the rub blend in white wine for a few minutes while you get everything else arranged lets the flavors bloom even more. Pasta on the Traeger—probably not what you expected!

Preheat your Traeger grill to 180°F (82°C), and turn on the Super Smoke feature if your grill has it. While the grill heats up, cook the pasta according to the package instructions until al dente. Drain it and set aside.

In a large bowl, toss the shrimp with the olive oil, then place them in the hot grill to smoke for 8 minutes. You don't want the shrimp to cook through (the shrimp will finish cooking in the sauce); rather, the goal is to infuse the shrimp with some wood-fired flavor.

While the shrimp smoke, in a small bowl, combine 2 teaspoons (6 g) of the Garlic Junky seasoning with the white wine, to allow the spices to bloom. After 8 minutes in the smoker, remove the shrimp and increase the temperature of your grill to 450°F (232°C). Place a cast-iron skillet in the grill to heat up.

When the skillet is very hot, add the butter and stir in the remaining 2 teaspoons (6 g) of the Garlic Junky seasoning. Add the shrimp to the hot skillet and cook for 1 to 2 minutes, until they just start to turn pink. Flip the shrimp and stir in the wine-seasoning mixture, the lemon juice and red pepper flakes. Continue cooking for 5 more minutes, until the sauce reduces and the shrimp is cooked through. Stir in the cooked pasta and toss to combine. Top with the parsley and season with salt and pepper to taste.

FAST HACK! If you don't have my Garlic Junky seasoning, you can substitute with the following for a copycat experience: Mix together 3 minced garlic cloves, 1 tablespoon (18 g) of kosher salt, 1 tablespoon (10 g) of garlic powder and 1 tablespoon (7 g) of fresh black pepper.

SEARED TUNA STEAKS WITH SPICY BOK CHOY

COOK TIME
15 minutes

YIELD
2 servings

PELLET
Any

TECHNIQUE
Hot & Fast (page 19)

EQUIPMENT
Pastry brush
Cast-iron skillet or griddle

INGREDIENTS
2 tbsp (30 ml) soy sauce
½ tsp honey
1 tsp kosher salt
1 tsp freshly ground black pepper
½ tsp garlic powder
¼ tsp cayenne pepper
2 (6–8-oz [170–227-g]) tuna steaks
1 tbsp (15 ml) vegetable oil
1 garlic clove, minced
½ tsp red pepper flakes
3 (4-oz [113-g]) heads of baby bok choy, trimmed and quartered

A perfectly cooked tuna steak is a can't-beat meal. After brushing it with soy sauce and seasoning it, tuna cooks very quickly on the grill. A high-quality tuna steak should have a strong sear on the edges and bright, rare flesh in the middle. For us, this is a great alternative to some of the heavier grilled dishes in the cookbook. We enjoy it with rice and fresh sauteed veggies like the baby bok choy in this recipe.

Preheat your Traeger grill to 450°F (232°C). Place a cast-iron skillet or griddle in the grill to heat up.

In a small bowl, combine the soy sauce and honey and mix well. In a second small bowl, combine the salt, black pepper, garlic powder and cayenne pepper. With a pastry brush, brush the tuna steaks with a light coating of the soy sauce mixture on both sides. Then season the tuna steaks on all sides with the salt mixture.

Place the tuna steaks in the hot cast-iron skillet, and cook for 1 minute and 30 seconds per side. This will create a nice crust with a cool, rare center. Remove the tuna from the grill and cover loosely with foil.

Using the same skillet, heat the vegetable oil and add the minced garlic and red pepper flakes. Cook for about 1 minute, until just fragrant, and toss in the bok choy. Cook, stirring frequently, for about 5 minutes, until the the bok choy is bright green and crisp-tender.

Cut the tuna into slices and serve with the bok choy.

FAST TIP! You can ask your fishmonger for sushi-grade tuna, which will give you the best results. Fresh tuna like this can also be diced and made into poke!

GRILLED SCALLOPS IN CITRUS MOJO MARINADE

COOK TIME

10 minutes (plus 15 minutes to marinate)

YIELD

2–3 servings

PELLET

Any

TECHNIQUE

Hot & Fast (page 19)

EQUIPMENT

Cast-iron griddle or skillet

Shallow glass baking dish with a cover (or plastic wrap), for marinating

Pastry brush

Digital probe thermometer

INGREDIENTS

Zest and juice of 1 orange

Zest and juice of 1 lime

1 tbsp (15 ml) sesame oil

2 tbsp (30 ml) vegetable oil, plus extra for brushing onto the scallops

1 tbsp (15 ml) soy sauce

1 tsp finely chopped habanero pepper

2 garlic cloves, minced

½ tbsp (3 g) confectioners' sugar

12 large sea scallops

Scallops are delicious cooked quickly on your Traeger grill. This easy marinade would work well with any kind of seafood, but imparts a particularly nice citrusy flavor to scallops. Don't be surprised by the confectioners' sugar in the recipe—it counters the tang of the citrus and actually helps create a great sear on the scallops. I recommend using a cast-iron griddle or skillet in your grill for this cook, so you don't have to worry about losing your scallops in the grates.

Preheat your Traeger grill to 450°F (232°C). Place a cast-iron skillet in the grill to heat up for at least 15 minutes.

In a shallow glass baking dish, combine the orange zest and juice, lime zest and juice, sesame oil, vegetable oil, soy sauce, habanero pepper, garlic and confectioners' sugar and mix well. Add the scallops, cover and place in the fridge to marinate for about 15 minutes.

Remove the scallops from the marinade and dab away excess moisture from each side with a paper towel. Discard the marinade. Use a pastry brush to brush both sides of the scallops with a very small amount of vegetable oil, then place them in the hot cast-iron skillet. Cook the scallops for 3 minutes per side, until the internal temperature reaches 145°F (63°C). You should have a good brown sear on each side, and the meat should be just opaque and slightly firm. Be careful not to overcook the scallops, or they will become too firm and rubbery. Serve immediately and enjoy!

FIRE-ROASTED WHOLE FISH

COOK TIME
20 minutes

YIELD
Serves 4

PELLET
Any

TECHNIQUE
Outdoor Oven (page 21)

EQUIPMENT
Kitchen twine
Digital probe thermometer

INGREDIENTS
2 whole (1-lb [454-g]) fish, cleaned and descaled

3 tbsp (45 ml) olive oil or melted butter

2 tbsp (36 g) kosher salt

2 tbsp (14 g) freshly ground black pepper

1 lemon, sliced into rounds, plus cut lemon wedges for serving

2 garlic cloves, minced

8 sprigs fresh dill

8 sprigs fresh parsley

8 sprigs fresh tarragon

Not only is this an easy way to prepare fish, but it makes for a dramatic finish. We like using striped bass or branzino, but the recipe complements sea bass, red snapper and trout (pictured) equally well. Ask your fishmonger for their recommendation and use this technique to put a few whole grilled fish on the table in under an hour.

Preheat your Traeger grill to 375°F (191°C). Rinse the fish, inside and out, and pat dry with a paper towel. Place the fish on a cutting board and drizzle both fish with olive oil or melted butter inside and out. Then season the insides and outsides generously with salt and pepper.

Stuff the cavity of each fish with the lemon slices, garlic, dill, parsley and tarragon, dividing the ingredients evenly between the two fish. Tie several pieces of kitchen twine around the fish, securing the filling inside.

Place the fish directly on the grate. Cook for 15 to 20 minutes, depending on the size of your fish. For these trout, it took about 20 minutes of total cooking time. The flesh, when cooked, should be opaque and flaky, registering an internal temperature of about 145°F (63°C). Remove the fish from the grill, transfer them to a platter and snip the twine to release the aromatic filling. Serve with extra lemon wedges on the side.

LOW(ISH) & SLOW(ISH) BBQ TO FIT YOUR BUSY LIFE

As noted in the Introduction, I couldn't omit traditional BBQ favorites from this book just because their cook times are longer. So I have adapted some classics to better suit our busy lives. As a schoolteacher, there is nothing I like more than the change of pace that grilling on my Traeger provides. After a crazy week teaching hundreds of elementary school kids coding, programming and engineering, it's really fun to slow down, be methodical and cook up an amazing BBQ dish for us to enjoy with family and friends. But even I don't want to be tethered to the grill all weekend, so these sped-up solutions make BBQ classics more approachable. If you have a little extra time, you can start these recipes at 225°F (107°C) with your grill's Super Smoke feature enabled to give the dish a stronger smoky base. But certainly, follow the directions and crank up the heat later in the cook so you can get dinner on the table during daylight!

TRADITIONAL PULLED PORK SHOULDER

COOK TIME
4½ hours (plus 30 minutes to sweat and 1 hour to rest)

YIELD
6–8 servings

PELLET
Cherry

TECHNIQUE
Low(ish) & Slow(ish) (page 21)

EQUIPMENT
Digital probe thermometer
Aluminum foil pan

INGREDIENTS
1 (8-lb [3.6-kg]) bone-in pork shoulder
2 tbsp (30 ml) hot sauce
½ cup (64 g) pork rub, such as Pork & Poultry by Traeger
4 tbsp (56 g) unsalted butter, cut into pats
¼ cup (60 ml) agave syrup

FOR SERVING (OPTIONAL)
Hamburger or brioche buns, 1 per person
Prepared coleslaw, about ¼ cup (30 g) per person
BBQ sauce of your choice, about 2 tbsp (30 ml) per person

Pork shoulder is an amazing cut to cook in your smoker. It can feed large amounts of people, and it freezes well in smaller portions to be used for superfast weeknight meals. The sky is the limit when it comes to dishes that can use pulled pork—from baked potatoes and green chili to sandwiches and burgers. Once you try pulled pork on your Traeger, you won't want to make it any other way! A normal slow-smoked pork shoulder can take nine hours or more on the grill. But with my method, you can get equally delicious and tender results in less than half the time by increasing the temperature at which you cook the pork.

Place the pork shoulder on a cutting board, and pat it dry with a paper towel. Using a small sharp knife, score the fat cap side of the pork shoulder about ¼ inch (6 mm) deep in opposite directions, making a diamond pattern. This will make for more surface area (and a great bark) and helps render the fat as the pork cooks.

Preheat your Traeger grill to 350°F (177°C). Allow it to heat up for at least 15 minutes with the lid closed.

Meanwhile, apply the hot sauce to all sides of the pork shoulder, then season it thoroughly with the rub. Let the meat sweat on the counter after being seasoned for about 30 minutes. This allows the moisture in the meat to begin to absorb the flavor, which will help carry the seasoning deeper into the roast. When the meat is glistening after sweating, it's ready to take in smoke flavor from your Traeger.

Place the pork shoulder on the grill with the fat cap side up. Cook the pork shoulder for about 2 hours until it reaches an internal temperature of 160°F (71°C).

Remove the pork from the grill, place it in the foil pan and top it with the butter and agave syrup. Increase the heat on the Traeger to 375°F (191°C). Cover the pan with foil and place it back on the grill. Cook the pork shoulder for another 2 hours, or until the pork is probe tender—usually when it reaches an internal temperature of 198 to 204°F (92 to 96°C). When you can slide a meat thermometer into the meat and feel little resistance, remove the pan from the grill, open the foil to let some of the steam out and then wrap it tightly again in foil before resting the meat for 1 hour in an empty cooler before shredding. To serve as sandwiches, pile the buns with the pulled pork, top with the coleslaw and drizzle with the BBQ sauce.

FAST HACK! Package up the leftover shredded pork in smaller portions in vacuum or freezer bags and freeze for later. To reheat, simply submerge the sealed bag in boiling water for 10 to 15 minutes before serving.

SMOKY PORK BELLY BURNT ENDS

COOK TIME
3½ hours (plus 15 minutes to sweat)

YIELD
6–8 servings

PELLET
Apple

TECHNIQUE
Low(ish) & Slow(ish) (page 21)

EQUIPMENT
Baking sheet

Grill-proof wire rack (optional)

Spray bottle

Digitial probe thermometer

Aluminum foil pan

Toothpicks (optional, for serving)

INGREDIENTS
1 (5-lb [2.3-kg]) piece of pork belly with skin removed

¼ cup (32 g) pork rub, such as Double Smoke by Spiceology

½ cup (120 ml) apple juice

4 tbsp (56 g) unsalted butter, cut into pats

½ cup (120 ml) BBQ sauce, like the Kitchen Sink BBQ Sauce (page 158)

¼ cup (60 ml) honey

Pork belly burnt ends have become a big thing in the BBQ world in the last decade. You used to only be able to get brisket burnt ends at BBQ joints, and quantities were always limited. Plus, traditional burnt ends can take up to a dozen hours to prepare—because you have to cook the brisket first. But ever since someone discovered that you could cook pork belly in a similar way—low(ish) and slow(ish) until they're tender and succulent and coated in BBQ sauce—people like me have become full converts. I love how the point of a brisket tastes, so rather than cube it up for burnt ends, we make pork belly burnt ends to fill that desire. This will become one of your favorite dishes to BBQ in no time. Family and friends will love this dish and ask for it again and again. They can definitely be made ahead of time—like on the weekend—and then refrigerated to enjoy with your meals throughout the week. To reheat, place the burnt ends in a grill-proof pan with a little apple juice, cover in foil and heat in a 350°F (177°C) grill for about 20 minutes until heated through.

Preheat your Traeger grill to 275°F (135°C). While the grill preheats, cube the pork belly into 1-inch (2.5-cm) cubes. Place the cubes on a baking sheet, season all sides of the cubes with the rub and allow the meat to sweat on the baking sheet for about 15 minutes.

If your pork cubes are on the small side or the spaces between your grill grates are too big (and the pork would fall through the gaps), put the pork belly cubes on a grill-proof wire rack. Otherwise, place the pork belly directly on the grates in the grill. If you want to catch the drippings to make cleanup easier, place a baking sheet with aluminum foil under the shelf with the pork belly.

Transfer the apple juice to a spray bottle. Cook the pork for about 3 hours until it reaches an internal temperature of 195°F (91°C). Every 30 minutes during the cook, use the bottle to spritz the pork with apple juice to keep the cubes from drying out.

Once the pork reaches temperature, place the pork belly in the foil pan with the butter, BBQ sauce and honey. Stir it all together and place the pan back in the Traeger at 350°F (177°C) for about 30 minutes. You want the sauce to reduce and get caramelized a bit. The pork belly burnt ends will be tender and succulent. Once you achieve this result, remove the pan from the grill, transfer the pork belly pieces to a serving platter and serve with toothpicks if you'd like.

CHUCK ROAST BURNT ENDS

COOK TIME
3½ hours

YIELD
6–8 servings

PELLET
Signature

TECHNIQUE
Low(ish) & Slow(ish) (page 21)

EQUIPMENT
Digital probe thermometer
Aluminum foil pan

INGREDIENTS
1 (3-lb [1.5-kg]) chuck roast

¼ cup (32 g) of beef rub, such as Double Smoke by Spiceology

4 tbsp (56 g) unsalted butter, cut into pats

½ cup (120 ml) BBQ sauce (see recipes on pages 158–161)

2 tbsp (30 ml) hot sauce

Often called "poor man's burnt ends," there is nothing poor about these. They have an amazingly rich flavor and will become a staple in your cooking routine. Usually, burnt ends come from the point of the brisket, and this technique is both faster and more cost-effective.

Preheat your Traeger grill to 300°F (149°C).

Season the chuck roast liberally on all sides with the beef rub. Place the roast on the grill, and cook for about 2 hours, until the internal temperature reaches 160°F (71°C). When it reaches this benchmark, remove it from the grill and wrap it in foil.

Return the wrapped chuck roast to the Traeger, and cook for 1 more hour, until the internal temperature reaches 190°F (88°C).

Remove the chuck roast from the grill, and transfer it to a cutting board. Increase the Traeger's heat to 350°F (177°C). Using a large knife, cut the meat into 1-inch (2.5-cm) cubes. Place the cubes in the foil pan with the butter, BBQ sauce and hot sauce and mix to coat.

Place the pan with the meat in the grill and cook it for 30 minutes. The sauce should reduce a lot, and the cubes will be tender and succulent. Serve with your favorite BBQ sides and white bread for an entrée or with toothpicks for an appetizer.

QUICKER WHOLE SMOKED BRISKET

COOK TIME
5-7 hours (plus 1-6 hours to rest)

YIELD
6-8 servings

PELLET
Hickory or signature

TECHNIQUE
Low(ish) & Slow(ish) (page 21)

EQUIPMENT
Boning knife
Temperature probe (included in most Traeger models)
Spray bottle
Pink butcher paper

INGREDIENTS
1 full (about 12-lb [5-kg]) packer brisket
½ cup (144 g) kosher salt
½ cup (64 g) course ground black pepper (16 mesh)
½ cup (120 ml) beef broth

Brisket is often an intimidating cook to many home pitmasters. Normally, a whole brisket takes 12 to 14 hours (or more) to cook on the Traeger, but my recipe speeds this up to 5 to 7 hours. Using this recipe, you will be wowing your friends and family in no time. While a whole packer brisket is a fairly large cook, you can use the leftovers to make burritos, chili, sandwiches and more. I highly encourage you to try out a full cook—the more fatty point and the leaner, tender flat—so you can get the best of brisket.

Preheat your Traeger grill to 300°F (149°C). Allow it to heat up for at least 20 minutes with the lid closed.

Trimming a brisket seems overwhelming at first, but don't let it scare you. After a couple of brisket cooks, you will have it down. Start by trimming the fat cap side of the brisket with the boning knife. What you are trying to do is leave about ¼ inch (6 mm) of fat all over the brisket. It's best to trim the hard fat off because that will not render down during the cook. The goal is to make the brisket as even as possible to afford an efficient cooking process. Flaps or pieces that stick out can be cut off and saved for burgers or other cooks.

After trimming the fat cap side, flip the brisket over so the meat side is facing up. There will be a good amount of silver skin and fat to deal with. Remove the hard fat and silver skin that is easy to tackle. Like the fat cap side, you want a nice even surface to apply the rub to.

For a traditional brisket cook, season the meat with a 50/50 blend of salt and pepper. Apply generously to the whole brisket.

Place the brisket fat side down on the Traeger. Insert a temperature probe into the thickest part of the point of the brisket.

Cook for 3 to 4 hours, until the brisket reaches an internal temperature of around 160 to 170°F (71 to 77°C).

Transfer the beef broth to a spray bottle. When the brisket reaches this first temperature benchmark, spritz it with a little beef broth and then wrap it tightly in pink butcher paper. Then wrap the entire package tightly in aluminum foil. The paper wrap helps preserve the bark you've built on the brisket, while the aluminum foil keeps the moisture in the package to help accelerate the cook. When you're wrapping the brisket, increase the grill temperature to 350°F (177°C).

(continued)

QUICKER WHOLE SMOKED BRISKET (CONTINUED)

Return the wrapped brisket to the Traeger and continue cooking for about 2 more hours total. During this time, check the internal temperature of the thickest part of the brisket every 20 to 30 minutes, until the point reaches about 200°F (93°C). You want to achieve probe tenderness—when you can slide a thermometer into the meat and feel little resistance. The finish temperature should be between 198°F (92°C) and 204°F (96°C), depending upon the meat, the altitude where you're cooking and the ambient temperature, etc. Just remember to keep checking the internal temperature toward the end to achieve perfect results!

When the temperature probe slides easily into the brisket, remove it from the grill and open the foil to release some steam for 5 to 7 minutes. Then wrap it back up and place it in an empty cooler with several towels to rest for at least 1 hour, and up to 6.

To slice it, separate the brisket into two sections. The first slice is down the middle where the flat and point come together. Then slice the flat against the grain into nice pencil-width slices. For the point pieces, I rotate the meat and slice it against the grain into thicker slices. Serve immediately and enjoy!

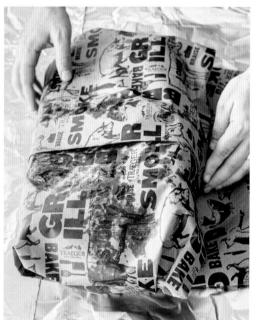

FAST HACKS! You don't often find brisket recipes that call for wrapping in both paper and aluminum foil. My friend Erik taught me this trick—especially for quick brisket cooks—because it helps trap the hot moisture in the package without degrading the bark. We call this the "Colorado crunch."

Also, don't throw out the juices that accumulate in the aluminum foil when you are cooking your brisket. If you separate the fat from the liquid, you are left with delicious beef concentrate. Use for soups, rehydrating leftover meat or whenever some beef broth is needed in a recipe.

SMOKED PORK RIBS

COOK TIME

4 hours (plus 15 minutes to
sweat and 15 minutes to rest)

YIELD

4–6 servings

PELLET

Cherry

TECHNIQUE

Low(ish) & Slow(ish) (page 21)

EQUIPMENT

Boning knife (for spareribs)

Pastry brush

Digital probe thermometer

Spray bottle

INGREDIENTS

2 racks of ribs (baby backs
weigh about 2 lbs [980 g] per
rack, and spareribs weigh
closer to 4 lbs [2 kg] per rack)

½ cup (120 ml) hot sauce

1 cup (128 g) pork rub, such as
Double Smoke by Spiceology
(see also the Perfect Pork Rub
recipe on page 17)

½ cup (120 ml) apple juice

½ cup (120 ml) agave syrup

½ cup (120 g) raw sugar

8 tbsp (112 g) unsalted butter,
cut into pats

1 cup (240 ml) BBQ sauce,
such as Head Country's
Original sauce

When making Traeger-smoked baby back or spareribs, you just cannot go wrong. Spareribs come from the belly area of the pig, while the baby backs come from the loin area. Baby backs tend to be leaner and more tender. Spares will have more marbling, which means more flavor but also a little longer cooking time to break down that marbling and make a tender bite. I recommend trying both and seeing what you and your family like best. Other than trimming and squaring the spareribs, the procedure for cooking both types of ribs is the same. Baby back ribs will cook about 30 minutes faster than spareribs. You'll often find people cook ribs on the Traeger with the 3-2-1 method—smoke for 3 hours, wrap for 2 hours and sauce and smoke for 1 hour—for a total of about 6 hours of cook time. I like this sped-up version, which produces equally amazing results in a little less time. There are lots of ways to cook ribs, but this technique has been the clear winner at our dinner table.

If you're using spareribs, use a sharp boning knife to trim each rack of spareribs to a more uniform shape. Trim the end bones off to leave 10 bones remaining, and square the meat on the long sides to be straighter and more even.

Preheat your Traeger grill to 225°F (107°C) and turn on the Super Smoke feature if your grill has it.

For both types of ribs, pull the silver skin membrane off the back of each rack. Use a small piece of paper towel to help you grip the skin on one edge and pull it off toward you. Then generously coat the ribs on both sides with hot sauce. Sprinkle the ribs liberally with the rub all over, and allow them to sweat on the counter for about 15 minutes as your grill heats up.

Place the seasoned ribs on the grill, meat side up, and cook until they reach an internal temperature of 160°F (71°C). It should take about 2½ hours. During the cook, pour the apple juice into a spray bottle. When checking the internal temperature, check how the ribs look too. If they appear dry during this part of the cook, use the spray bottle to spritz them with some apple juice.

(continued)

SMOKED PORK RIBS (CONTINUED)

Prepare a double layer of heavy-duty aluminum foil to wrap each rack of the ribs in. On each double layer of foil, drizzle one quarter of the agave, sprinkle with one quarter of the sugar and arrange one quarter of the butter pats. Once the ribs reach the first benchmark temperature, remove them from the grill and place them on the prepared foil, meat side down on the agave, sugar and butter. Top each rack of ribs with another quarter of the agave, sugar and butter pats, then wrap tightly in the foil. Keep the ribs meat side down in the foil wrap and then return the ribs to the grill to continue cooking. Increase the grill temperature to 275°F (135°C) and cook for about 1½ hours until the ribs reach an internal temperature of 204°F (96°C).

Remove the ribs from the grill and allow them to rest for 15 minutes. Carefully remove the ribs from the foil, and slice them into individual ribs. Serve with the BBQ sauce on the side.

FAST HACK! You can sauce your ribs before serving (rather than serving the sauce on the side) by glazing them when the internal temperature reaches about 195°F (91°C). If opting for sauced ribs, open the foil, carefully turn the ribs meat side up (leaving them nestled in the foil) and glaze with a 50/50 combination of your favorite BBQ sauce and Grill Candy by BurntOut BBQ. Return the foil packages to the grill, with the aluminum foil open, for about 15 minutes, until the internal temperature reaches 204°F (96°C). You will get an amazing shiny coating on the ribs that adds another dimension of flavor!

BEEF DINO BONES

COOK TIME
5–6 hours (plus 1 hour to rest)

YIELD
4–6 servings

PELLET
Mesquite

TECHNIQUE
Low(ish) & Slow(ish) (page 21)

EQUIPMENT
Boning knife
Digital probe thermometer
Pink butcher paper

INGREDIENTS
¼ cup (72 g) kosher salt
¼ cup (34 g) coarse ground black pepper (16 mesh)
1 set of beef plate ribs (usually a 3-bone set weighs about 8 lbs [3.5 kg])
2 tbsp (30 ml) hot sauce

One of the best BBQ bites I've ever had has to be beef ribs. I call it "brisket on a stick"—essentially rich and succulent beef that comes with a handle. One bite and you will fall in love. These are common at authentic Texas BBQ spots like Franklin BBQ, and with some practice, you can perfect this iconic cook at home. Beef ribs can easily take nine or more hours, and here I have sped up the cook time with a shorter initial smoke period that still gives great results. Feel free to experiment with a longer cook time at 225°F (107°C); this will infuse even more smoke flavor into the cook but also add a few extra hours of total cook time. I recommend ordering the ribs from a trusted meat source (I use Snake River Farms) or visiting your local butcher to get them. The dino bone cut is known as the 123A beef plate cut, which you may need to tell your butcher to be sure you get the right thing! Or simply order online, and it'll be easier than ever.

Preheat your Traeger grill to 225°F (107°C) and turn on the Super Smoke feature if your grill has it. Allow the grill to heat for at least 20 minutes while you prepare the ribs.

Combine the salt and pepper in a small bowl and set aside.

Then it's time to trim the beef ribs. This may seem like a daunting task, but it's actually not too bad and gets easier with every cook. Starting on the back side of the ribs, use a boning knife to score the membrane on the diagonal, then rotate 90 degrees and score again to create a diamond pattern. This helps the smoke get through the membrane and breaks it down during the cook.

Next, trim the meat side of the ribs. You want to take the hard fat off and leave a nice meaty surface where the bark will form. Try not to chase the fat and cut it all off. Instead, just focus on removing the fat on the surface that is hard and won't render off. The more you clear the surface of the meat, the better bark you'll develop as you cook.

Season your ribs by first coating them in a thin layer of hot sauce and then an even coating of the salt and pepper mixture.

Place the ribs on the Traeger, meat side up, and cook them for 1 hour to give them a good smoky base. Then increase the grill temperature to 275°F (135°C) and continue cooking the ribs for about 2 more hours.

When the ribs reach an internal temperature of about 165°F (74°C), remove them from the grill and wrap them tightly in pink butcher paper.

(continued)

BEEF DINO BONES (CONTINUED)

Return the wrapped ribs to the grill and continue cooking them at 275°F (135°C) until they are probe tender. Depending on the meat, this will occur when the internal temperature is about 204 to 210°F (95 to 99°C) internally. It should take another 2 to 3 hours to reach this temperature range.

Once the ribs are probe tender, remove them from the grill. Keeping them wrapped in the paper, wrap the package in towels, place the bundle in an empty cooler and let the meat rest for at least 1 hour.

When you're ready to serve, unwrap the ribs and cut them into individual bones. This makes an amazing presentation for your family and guests.

PORK ROAST WITH MUSTARD & CRANBERRIES

COOK TIME
3 hours (plus 15–20 minutes to rest)

YIELD
4–6 servings

PELLET
Cherry or pecan

TECHNIQUE
Reverse Sear (page 19)

EQUIPMENT
Roasting pan with a rack
Digital probe thermometer

INGREDIENTS
1 whole (about 6-lb [2.7-kg]) bone-in rack of pork

½ cup (120 ml) plus 2 tbsp (30 ml) spicy English mustard, divided (I like Colman's)

½ cup (120 ml) apple cider, divided

½ cup (46 g) finely chopped assorted fresh herbs (such as a combination of rosemary, thyme, parsley and sage), plus a handful of whole fresh herbs for the roasting pan

Kosher salt, divided

2 celery ribs, cut into 2-inch (5-cm) pieces

2 apples, diced into ¼-inch (6-mm) cubes (I like Honeycrisp)

2 yellow onions, quartered

2 cups (220 g) fresh cranberries

½ cup (120 ml) chicken broth

1 tbsp (14 g) cornstarch

3 tbsp (45 ml) cold water

Freshly ground black pepper

Roasted or grilled vegetables and/or mashed potatoes, for serving

For this easy family meal, we created an impressive dish with little effort. Start with a delicious whole rack of pork and season it with a flavorful herb and mustard mixture. It's roasted in the Traeger grill until a good crust develops, and a pan sauce of apples, cranberries and herbs makes an awesome accompaniment. A pork roast like this is essentially the equivalent to a prime rib, and while it might normally be considered perfect for a holiday meal, it can be great for a weekend meal with leftovers to use in a variety of ways throughout the week. With my method, you will give the roast a great smoky base and then bump up the temperature to get dinner on the table in less time. The crust that comes from the high heat and mustard paste is incredibly delicious.

Preheat your Traeger grill to 250°F (121°C) while you prepare the rack of pork.

Begin by removing the silver skin membrane from the back of the ribs. Use a small piece of paper towel to get a grip on one edge of the membrane and then pull it off toward you.

Next, make the mustard paste to season the meat. In a bowl, combine the ½ cup (120 ml) of mustard, ¼ cup (60 ml) of apple cider, the chopped herbs and a pinch of salt. Stir together until the ingredients are well mixed. The mixture will be slightly runny.

Apply the mustard mixture all over the rack of pork. I like to let it sit on the pork for about 15 minutes to let the flavors saturate the meat. Ensure the top of the roast has a visible layer of mustard paste. In a roasting pan, place the celery, apples, onions, cranberries, whole herbs, remaining apple cider and chicken broth. Distribute evenly. Place a roasting rack in the pan and place the pork roast on it.

Place the pan in the grill. Cook until the internal temperature reaches about 130°F (54°C). For my 6-pound (2.7-kg) roast, it took about 2½ hours, and I started checking the temperature after about 1½ hours.

(continued)

PORK ROAST WITH MUSTARD & CRANBERRIES (CONTINUED)

Once the roast reaches an internal temperature of 130°F (54°C), remove the roasting pan from the grill. Transfer the pork to a platter and loosely tent with foil. Meanwhile, increase the grill temperature to 450°F (232°C). Once the grill is up to temperature, return the roast to the grill, placing it directly on the grates, and sear it for 10 to 15 minutes, until the internal temperature is nearly 145°F (63°C) and the crust has browned all over. Return the pork to the platter, tent with foil again and allow it to rest for about 15 to 20 minutes.

While the roast is searing, fish out the onion quarters, celery pieces and herb stems from the roasting pan and discard. Pour the remaining apples, cranberries and juices into a small saucepan. Bring the pan juices to a simmer on the stove. Whisk the remaining 2 tablespoons (30 ml) of mustard into the pan. In a small bowl, combine the cornstarch with cold water, mix well, and whisk into the pan to help thicken the sauce. It will be the texture of a chutney. Season with salt and pepper to taste and transfer to a serving dish.

Slice the pork roast into individual chops between the ribs. Serve with the cranberry-mustard pan sauce and the vegetables and mashed potatoes if you'd like.

ORANGE-MAPLE GLAZED HAM

COOK TIME

2½ hours (plus 20 minutes to rest)

YIELD

8-10 servings

PELLET

Any

TECHNIQUE

Outdoor Oven (page 21)

EQUIPMENT

Small grill-proof saucepan

Roasting pan to fit the ham

Digital probe thermometer

HAM

1 half bone-in ham (about 9 lbs [4 kg])

½ cup (60 g) pork rub, such as Double Smoke by Spiceology

GLAZE

Juice of 2 oranges (about 1 cup [240 ml])

½ cup (120 ml) maple syrup

¼ cup (60 ml) Dijon mustard

2 tbsp (30 ml) apple cider vinegar

1 cup (240 ml) apricot jam

2 tsp (10 ml) hot sauce

Many families reserve dishes like a glazed ham for holiday meals. But with the simplicity of cooking on the Traeger, you'll soon find that some of those laborious cooks are quite easy and fun when you're cooking outdoors. We make a bone-in ham like this throughout the year, as it's a delicious family meal and the leftovers are extremely versatile. From sandwiches for lunches to easy weeknight meals, it's great to have ham on hand that has been glazed and smoked in the Traeger. As with the Traditional Pulled Pork Shoulder (page 94), you can package up leftovers in freezer bags and get dinner on the table in no time later on!

Preheat your Traeger grill to 325°F (163°C) while you prepare the ham and the glaze.

Begin by scoring the skin side of the ham in a diamond pattern. Cut about ½ inch (1.3 cm) deep. This provides more surface area for the rub and the glaze to stick to during the cook, which ensures you get an amazing crust. After scoring, season the ham all over with the pork rub.

To make the glaze, in a small, grill-proof saucepan, combine the orange juice, maple syrup, Dijon mustard, apple cider vinegar, apricot jam and hot sauce. Place the saucepan in the grill to warm. Put the ham in the roasting pan and then transfer the pan to the grill. Cook the ham for 45 minutes, stirring the sauce occasionally. After 45 minutes, pour a third of the glaze over the ham. Allow to cook for another 45 minutes, then glaze the ham again with half of what's left.

At the 2-hour mark, glaze the ham with the remaining glaze and continue cooking until the ham reaches an internal temperature of 140°F (60°C). For a 9-pound (4-kg) ham, this will be about 2½ hours total.

Remove the ham from the grill and allow it to rest for 20 minutes before slicing and serving with some of the glaze from the bottom of the pan on the side.

PRIME RIB ROAST

COOK TIME
2½ hours (plus 25 minutes to rest)

YIELD
6–8 servings

PELLET
Hickory

TECHNIQUE
Reverse Sear (page 19)

EQUIPMENT
Boning knife (for a bone-in prime rib)

Butcher twine (for a bone-in prime rib)

Digital probe thermometer

PRIME RIB
1 (8–10-lb (3.6–4.5-kg) bone-in or boneless prime rib

½ cup (64 g) beef rub, such as Garlic Junky or Coffee Junky by Spiceology

HORSERADISH SAUCE
½ cup (120 ml) sour cream

½ cup (120 ml) mayonnaise

½ cup (120 ml) prepared extra hot horseradish (from a jar)

Juice of ½ a lemon

Kosher salt

Freshly ground black pepper

Nothing says family dinner and an important holiday meal more than a perfectly cooked prime rib. By reverse searing the roast, you will first impart delicious smoky flavor to the meat and then give it that amazing, distinctive crust with the final cook at high heat in your Traeger. We love to serve this dish with homemade horseradish sauce and Smoky Yorkshire Puddings (page 137).

Preheat your Traeger grill to 225°F (107°C) and turn on the Super Smoke feature if your grill has it.

If you are using a boneless prime rib, skip ahead to the next step. For a bone-in prime rib, use a boning knife to cut along the rib plate and remove the bulk of the meat in one piece from the bones. Cut along the curve of the bones as you separate the pieces, leaving the bone plate intact as one piece. Season the cut sides generously with the rub and use butcher twine to tie the bone plate back on the roast.

Season all sides of the roast generously with the rub, patting to adhere the rub evenly across all surfaces. Place the roast on the grill and cook for 30 minutes to get a great smoky base. Then increase the grill temperature to 275°F (135°C), cooking until the internal temperature reaches 115°F (46°C) in the center for medium-rare. Remember that it will continue cooking during the final sear. Start checking the internal temperature after the first hour, then check every 15 minutes. It should take about 90 minutes for the internal temperature to reach 115°F (46°C).

Remove the the roast from the grill and tent with foil while you increase the grill temperature to 450°F (232°C) for searing. Once the grill is up to temperature, place the roast back on the grill and cook for about 15 to 20 minutes, until the meat reaches an internal temperature of 125°F (52°C) for medium-rare. Transfer the roast to a cutting board and again tent with foil. Allow it to rest for at least 25 minutes before slicing.

Make the horseradish sauce while the roast rests. In a small bowl, combine the sour cream, mayonnaise, horseradish and lemon juice, and mix until well blended. Season with salt and pepper to taste.

If you have a bone-in prime rib, snip the butcher twine and place the bones to the side. Carve the roast into ¾-inch (2-cm)-thick slices and serve with the sauce.

FAST HACK! Carving a whole bone-in prime rib can be challenging, so I like to cut off the rib bones ahead of cooking and then tie them back on. Not only does this add more flavor to your roast—with the seasoning added in between the meat and bones—but it also makes the prime rib extremely easy to carve when the cooking is done.

SMOKED LEG OF LAMB

COOK TIME
3 hours (plus 20 minutes to rest)

YIELD
6–8 servings

PELLET
Cherry or pecan

TECHNIQUE
Low(ish) & Slow(ish) (page 21)

EQUIPMENT
Blender or food processor
Pastry brush
Digital probe thermometer

INGREDIENTS
1 (5–7-lb [2.3–3.25-kg]) upper sirloin bone-in leg of lamb
½ cup (120 ml) olive oil
5 tbsp (70 ml) lemon juice
Zest of 1 lemon
⅓ cup (80 ml) Dijon mustard
8 garlic cloves
1 handful each of fresh thyme, parsley and rosemary
2 shallots
2 tbsp (36 g) kosher salt
2 tbsp (14 g) coarse ground black pepper (16 mesh)

This is a recipe that would be an amazing centerpiece for a holiday meal with family. However, cooking on the Traeger is so fun and easy that you could mix this into your rotation for special dinners. If you leave a bit of the fat on the top of the leg, you will end up with really tender and juicy meat, as the fat renders during this slow(ish) cook. The addition of the herb sauce complements the flavor of the lamb. It could normally take five or more hours to make this dish, but a slightly higher temperature produces equally tender results in less time. I recommend using the upper sirloin piece of a leg of lamb for this recipe.

Preheat your Traeger grill to 250°F (121°C). While the grill preheats, bring the leg of lamb to room temperature.

In a blender or food processor, combine the olive oil, lemon juice, lemon zest, mustard, garlic, thyme, parsley, rosemary and shallots and blend until smooth. Transfer the sauce to a bowl and season it with salt and pepper to taste. It should be pungent. Reserve and refrigerate a third of the prepared herb sauce. Brush the leg of lamb with the remaining sauce and place it directly on the grill.

Cook the lamb for 1 hour, then begin checking the internal temperature. Continue the process of checking the temperature every 30 minutes for the remainder of the cook. Allow the lamb to cook for about 3 hours, until the internal temperature reaches 145°F (73°C).

Remove the leg of lamb from the grill and transfer it to a cutting board. Tent with foil and allow it to rest for 20 minutes before slicing. Serve with the reserved herb sauce on the side.

FAST HACK! Your local butcher should be able to provide you with a bone-in leg of lamb, or you can order one online from retailers like Superior Farms that will ship directly to your home. You could also use a boneless leg of lamb with this same recipe and decrease the cooking time by about 1 hour.

SMOKED SPATCHCOCK TURKEY

COOK TIME
3½–4 hours (plus 12 hours for brining and 20 minutes to rest)

YIELD
4–6 servings

PELLET
Signature

TECHNIQUE
Outdoor Oven (page 21)

EQUIPMENT
Kitchen shears and/or cleaver knife

Baking sheet with a wire rack

Pastry brush

Digital probe thermometer

DRY BRINE
5 tbsp (69 g) kosher salt

5 tbsp (15 g) dried herbs (such as thyme, sage, rosemary and parsley)

3 tbsp (21 g) coarse ground black pepper (16 mesh)

2 tbsp (10 g) red pepper flakes

Zest of 1 lemon

TURKEY
1 whole (8–12-lb [3.6–5.4-kg]) turkey, defrosted if frozen

FOR THE COOK
8 tbsp (112 g) Garlic Junky Compound Butter (page 162), melted and divided

My wife was a turkey traditionalist—she always believed that a turkey roasted in the oven was the best (and only) way to go. But once we got our Traeger and had a Thanksgiving with two turkeys—one in the oven and one on the grill—she became a convert. Cooking a turkey on the Traeger has a lot of benefits because the consistent convection cooking temperature of the grill produces a juicy, tender bird with an extra boost of wood-fired flavor. We dry brine our turkeys with a tasty blend of salt, pepper and spices, either homemade using the recipe to follow or a store-bought brine seasoning like The Fall Guy by Spiceology. You can do a traditional wet brine, but we find the results are actually better with a dry mixture, and there's a lot less to clean up. Be sure to spatchcock your bird so it cooks evenly. A spatchcocked turkey will also cook much more quickly than a traditional whole turkey. A great thing about cooking a turkey on the Traeger is that with a different kind of seasoning, such as a Cajun blend, you can start enjoying turkey year-round!

The day before you plan to serve the turkey, combine the dry brine ingredients in bowl. Mix to combine and set aside.

Place the turkey on a large cutting board and remove and discard the gizzards. Using sharp kitchen shears, remove the backbone from the turkey. Flip the bird cut side down on the board and press firmly to break the breast bone and flatten the bird. Pat the bird dry with paper towels.

Place the flattened turkey on a wire rack set over a baking sheet, and season both sides of the bird liberally with the dry brine mixture. Place it in the fridge, uncovered, for about 12 hours or overnight.

The day you're planning to serve your turkey, preheat your Traeger grill to 400°F (204°C). Remove the turkey from the fridge. Using a pastry brush, coat the skin side of the turkey generously with 4 tablespoons (60 ml) of the melted compound butter. Allow the bird to rest for 15 minutes while the grill preheats.

Place the spatchcocked turkey directly on the grates of the grill, skin side up. Take a moment to position the turkey so the legs are straight and the bird is as flat as possible.

Grill the turkey for 30 minutes at 400°F (204°C), then decrease the grill temperature to 325°F (163°C). After 1 hour, brush the bird with the remaining 4 tablespoons (60 ml) of melted compound butter. Cook for 2 to 2½ hours longer, checking the internal temperature of the thickest part of the breast with a digital probe thermometer after an hour, then every 20 minutes thereafter, until it reaches 165°F (74°C). Remove the turkey from the grill and allow it to rest for 20 minutes before carving and serving.

SMOKING
SIDES & APPS

It's really fun to cook a meal for family and friends and point out to them that every portion of the menu was cooked on the Traeger. These recipes are some of our favorite sides and starters that can be cooked alongside the main dish on the grill. Note that if you cook in a ceramic or stoneware baking dish instead of cast iron, the baking dish may come off the grill looking darker, but a quick scrub with dish soap afterward will bring it back to an almost-new sheen.

CAST-IRON SCALLOPED POTATOES

COOK TIME
35 minutes

YIELD
4–6 servings

PELLET
Any

TECHNIQUE
Outdoor Oven (page 21)

EQUIPMENT
10-inch (25-cm) cast-iron skillet

INGREDIENTS
1 tbsp (14 g) unsalted butter

½ white onion, minced

2 garlic cloves, minced

½ tsp fresh thyme

1 cup (240 ml) chicken broth

1 cup (240 ml) half & half

1½ lbs (680 g) yellow potatoes, sliced into ¼-inch (6-mm) rounds

4 oz (113 g) Swiss or Gruyère cheese, grated

Kosher salt

Freshly ground black pepper

These scalloped potatoes come together in one pan and are cheesy, creamy and have a strong garlic and thyme flavor. We start the sauce on the stove inside if we can, then transfer the pan once we add the potatoes to cook on the Traeger. This stretegy keeps your kitchen cool, and the potatoes can bake while your main dish finishes up on the grill at the same time.

Preheat your Traeger grill to 450°F (232°C). In a 10-inch (25-cm) cast-iron skillet on the stove, melt the butter over medium heat. Add the onion and cook for about 3 minutes, until it is just translucent. Stir in the garlic and thyme and cook for about 2 more minutes. Stir in the chicken broth and half & half and bring to a boil. Add the potatoes to the skillet and stir gently to submerge them in the liquid. Bring to a simmer, cover and cook for 10 minutes, stirring occasionally.

Sprinkle the potatoes with the cheese. Season with salt and pepper to taste. Carefully transfer the skillet to the grill and bake for 15 to 20 minutes until the potatoes are tender and the cheese is melty. Allow to stand for 5 minutes before serving.

BACON-WRAPPED ASPARAGUS

COOK TIME
15 minutes

YIELD
8 bundles (4 servings)

PELLET
Any

TECHNIQUE
Outdoor Oven (page 21)

EQUIPMENT
Grill-proof baking sheet
Parchment paper

INGREDIENTS
1 (1-lb [454-g]) bunch of asparagus, ends trimmed

8 bacon slices (we use thin-cut bacon, as it is easier to wrap with and cooks more quickly)

2 tsp (8 g) pork rub, such as Double Smoke by Spiceology

These bundles of asparagus spears wrapped in bacon cook quickly on a hot grill and are easy to serve alongside your main entrée. You could substitute green beans for a fun spin on this dish. In my opinion, everything is better with bacon!

Preheat your Traeger grill to 375°F (191°C).

Divide the asparagus into eight portions. Wrap each portion in a piece of bacon, spiraling the bacon around the spears so there isn't much overlap. Secure with toothpicks if necessary. Season lightly with the rub. Line a grill-proof baking sheet with parchment paper and carefully arrange the asparagus bundles on it, leaving a little space in between each one. For best results, turn the bundles so the ends of the bacon are tucked underneath and won't unravel.

Place the baking sheet in the grill and cook for about 15 minutes, until the bacon is crispy and the asparagus is tender. Serve immediately.

TRAEGER SKILLET VEGGIES

COOK TIME
25–30 minutes

YIELD
4 servings

PELLET
Pecan or cherry

TECHNIQUE
Outdoor Oven (page 21)

EQUIPMENT
Large grill-proof skillet

INGREDIENTS
6 cups (weight varies) mixed fresh vegetables, chopped into uniform pieces (we used 1 cup each of onion, purple and white cauliflower, asparagus tips, red bell pepper and butternut squash)

2 tbsp (30 ml) olive oil

1 tbsp (9 g) garlic powder

1 tbsp (7 g) onion powder

2 tbsp (36 g) kosher salt

2 tbsp (14 g) freshly ground black pepper

1 tbsp (7 g) paprika

This is an incredibly easy and delicious way to use up veggies in your fridge to serve with a grilled main dish. Choose any combination that suits you, or whatever you have on hand, and season the veggies with olive oil and a rub. When cooked on a hot grill, they will be done in about 30 minutes. If you use firmer vegetables like butternut squash, cut them into smaller pieces and extend the cook time a bit to allow the pieces to get tender. This will soon become one of your favorite ways to serve veggies from the Traeger, with that distinct, slightly smoky flavor that cooking with wood pellets provides.

Preheat your Traeger grill to 400°F (204°C). In a large bowl, combine the vegetables, olive oil, garlic powder, onion powder, salt, pepper and paprika. Toss to coat and then transfer the seasoned vegetables to a grill-proof skillet.

Place the skillet in the grill and allow the vegetables to roast for 15 minutes. Remove the skillet briefly to stir the vegetables and then place it back in the grill. Continue cooking for another 10 to 15 minutes, until the vegetables are tender and beginning to brown. Serve immediately with your grilled entrée.

SMOKED HASSELBACK POTATOES

COOK TIME
1 hour

YIELD
4 servings

PELLET
Pecan

TECHNIQUE
Outdoor Oven (page 21)

EQUIPMENT
Grill-proof bowl
Chopsticks
Pastry brush
Grill-proof baking sheet

INGREDIENTS
8 tbsp (112 g) unsalted butter

⅓ cup (16 g) chopped chives

4 large russet or sweet potatoes (8 oz [227 g] each)

½ lb (227 g) thick-cut bacon, chopped into 1-inch (2.5-cm) pieces

½ lb (227 g) cheddar cheese, shredded

This is a perfect side dish for those family dinners when you are looking for something a little different but still simple and full of flavor. The sky is the limit with the filling on these, but cheddar, bacon and chives harkens back to great traditional baked potatoes and makes for an unexpected presentation. To speed up your dinnertime prepwork, cut the potatoes the night before, then pop them on the grill when you're cooking the rest of your meal.

Preheat your Traeger grill to 425°F (218°C).

While the grill preheats, in a grill-proof bowl, melt the butter on the grill. Carefully remove the bowl, stir in the chives and set aside.

Position a potato between two chopsticks so there is one chopstick on each long side of the potato. Cut the potato into thin slices widthwise. The chopsticks will help you avoid cutting all the way through the potato. The cuts should stop about ¼ inch (6 mm) from the bottom.

Using your fingers, gently separate each potato slice and brush the melted chive butter between the slices. Place pieces of bacon between the slices. Repeat with the rest of the potatoes, dividing the bacon pieces evenly among all of the potatoes, then place the potatoes on a grill-proof baking sheet.

Bake on the grill for about 50 minutes, until the potatoes are tender in the middle and crisp around the edges. Sprinkle the potatoes with the cheese and bake for 5 more minutes until melted, then remove them from the grill and serve.

FAST HACKS! Did you know that potatoes are actually best cooked to temperature? For these, I would shoot for an internal temperature of 205°F (96°C).

A less labor-intensive alternative to the hasselback arrangement is whole baked potatoes on the grill. Coat russet potatoes generously in olive oil and salt and put them directly on the grates of your Traeger at 375°F (191°C) for about 45 minutes. Remove the potatoes from the grill when the internal temperature reaches 205°F (96°C)—you've never had a baked potato so creamy and delicious!

THE CHEESIEST ONE-PAN MACARONI & CHEESE

COOK TIME
1 hour 25 minutes

YIELD
6–8 servings

PELLET
Any

TECHNIQUE
Outdoor Oven (page 21)

EQUIPMENT
Grill-proof baking dish
(9 x 11 inches [23 x 28 cm]
or larger)
Blender or food processor

INGREDIENTS
3 tbsp (42 g) unsalted butter, divided

1 cup (225 g) cottage cheese

½ cup (123 g) ricotta cheese

2 cups (480 ml) milk

2 cups (480 ml) chicken broth

1 tbsp (7 g) ground mustard

1 tsp garlic powder

1 tsp onion powder

1 tbsp (15 ml) hot sauce

1½ lbs (680 g) cheddar cheese, shredded

16 oz (454 g) dry pasta (elbows, shells or bowties are great)

Macaroni and cheese is a very traditional accompaniment to great BBQ. This recipe simplifies the process of making this extra-cheesy dish by using only one pan for the cooking. Cleanup is supremely easy, and there's no need to make a roux and cheese sauce. Simply blend the sauce ingredients, pour it over uncooked pasta and throw it all in your Traeger to cook. Put the dish on the grill when you get home from work, and prep the rest of your meal while it cooks. Stir it a few times and you'll end up with the cheesiest macaroni and cheese possible.

Preheat your Traeger grill to 400°F (204°C). Use 1 tablespoon (14 g) of the butter to grease the bottom and sides of a grill-proof baking dish.

In a blender or food processor, combine the cottage cheese, ricotta cheese, milk, chicken broth, ground mustard, garlic powder, onion powder and hot sauce. Blend it on high until smooth and frothy. Stir in the shredded cheese and blend again briefly just to incorporate.

Add the dry pasta to the prepared baking dish. Pour the cheese mixture over the dry pasta and stir gently to combine. Spread evenly in the dish and cover tightly with aluminum foil.

Bake in the Traeger for 45 minutes, rotating the dish and stirring the contents once after 30 minutes. Continue cooking and check the pasta for doneness every 15 minutes until it is al dente, about 1 hour and 15 minutes total. Stir the mixture if parts look dry or the pasta has popped out of the sauce.

When the pasta is al dente, remove the foil cover, arrange bits of the remaining 2 tablespoons (28 g) of butter on top of pasta and return the baking dish to the grill, uncovered, for 10 more minutes until bubbly and golden. Serve immediately.

FAST HACK! This recipe could easily be made gluten free. Rather than making a roux for the cheese sauce, which traditionally has flour in it, this recipe uses the pasta to absorb the liquid from the mix, leaving behind the creamy melted cheese. Substitute gluten-free pasta and adjust the cook time based on when the pasta gets al dente.

EASY TRAEGER DUTCH BABY

COOK TIME
30 minutes

YIELD
4–6 servings

PELLET
Any

TECHNIQUE
Outdoor Oven (page 21)

EQUIPMENT
Cast-iron skillet or Dutch oven
Blender

INGREDIENTS
4 whole large eggs
1 egg yolk
¾ cup (94 g) flour
¾ cup (180 ml) milk
1 tbsp (18 g) kosher salt
1 tbsp (7 g) freshly ground
black pepper
4 tbsp (56 g) unsalted butter
Toppings of your choice (we
like warmed, chopped leftover
brisket, diced red onion and
BBQ sauce)

A Dutch baby cooked in your Traeger is a magical thing. Not only does it impressively puff up while cooking, but it can also be adapted to suit many different meals. I am a fan of the savory version of these pancakes to accompany grilled meat, but they can easily be made sweet to serve as a dessert or for breakfast. The sweet variation is delicious served with sliced fruit and whipped cream. See the Fast Hack for a sweet variation on this recipe!

Preheat your Traeger grill to 450°F (232°C). Place a cast-iron skillet in the grill to heat up.

In a blender, combine the eggs, egg yolk, flour, milk, salt and pepper. Blend for 1½ minutes until very smooth and frothy. When the grill and the skillet have preheated for 10 to 15 minutes, place the butter in the hot skillet and allow it to begin to brown and smell nutty. This should take about 3 minutes. Using an oven mitt, rotate the skillet to swirl the butter until the bottom is evenly coated, then pour the mixture from the blender directly into the hot butter.

Close the grill and allow it to heat back up to 450°F (232°C). Bake the Dutch baby for 20 minutes, checking only once after about 15 minutes. The edges should creep up the sides of the skillet, and the center will likely puff up like a balloon. After 20 minutes, decrease the grill temperature to 300°F (149°C) and cook for 5 more minutes. During this step, the puffed pancake will collapse, which is what it's supposed to do.

Remove the skillet from the heat, cut into wedges and serve immediately with your favorite toppings.

FAST HACK! For a sweet variation of a Dutch baby, use the same ingredients but include 1½ tablespoons (19 g) of sugar, ¼ teaspoon of cinnamon, ½ teaspoon of vanilla and a pinch of salt in place of the salt and pepper. Cook the same way, and serve with fruit and whipped cream.

GRILLED GARLIC JUNKY NAAN

As you have seen throughout this book, the Garlic Junky seasoning I developed with Spiceology can be used in a wide variety of recipes. This is one of my unexpected favorites because it's a fairly simple recipe that is the perfect accompaniment to any number of meats in this book. Naan is traditionally served with Indian food, but we use it as the vessel for sandwiches and wraps, as a mop for tasty sauces, as a side with grilled meats like the Smoked Leg of Lamb (page 117) and even the base for pizza. Make the dough ahead of time, and then, even on a busy weeknight, you can cook the breads quickly on a super hot cast-iron griddle just before serving your main dish. These tasty breads are incredibly tender and have that distinct Garlic Junky flavor that everyone loves.

COOK TIME
30–40 minutes (plus 30 minutes to let the dough rise)

YIELD
10 naan breads (10 servings)

PELLET
Any

TECHNIQUE
Hot & Fast (page 19)

EQUIPMENT
Stand mixer with a dough hook
Cast-iron skillet or griddle

INGREDIENTS
¼ cup (60 ml) warm water
1 tbsp (15 ml) honey
¾ tsp active dry yeast
¾ cup (180 ml) milk
1 cup (240 ml) Greek yogurt
4 cups (500 g) flour, plus more for kneading
1½ tsp (7 g) baking powder
1 tsp baking soda
¼ tsp kosher salt
4 tbsp (56 g) unsalted butter, divided
2 tbsp (26 g) Garlic Junky Seasoning by Spiceology (see Fast Hack)

In the bowl of a stand mixer, mix together the water, honey and yeast. Allow the mixture to sit for 10 minutes, until bubbly. Add the milk, yogurt, flour, baking powder, baking soda and salt. Mix for about 5 minutes with the dough hook attachment until well incorporated. Turn the dough out onto a well-floured work surface and knead for about 5 minutes, until it forms a smooth ball, using extra flour as needed. Transfer the dough back to the bowl and cover it with a towel. Allow the dough to rise for about 30 minutes.

Preheat your Traeger grill to 450°F (232°C). Place a cast-iron skillet in the grill to heat up. Meanwhile, transfer the risen dough to a work surface and divide it into 10 balls. Flatten each ball with a rolling pin until it is about ¼ inch (6 mm) thick. Dust each with flour, cover and set aside.

Using a microwave, melt half the butter in a small bowl. When the grill is hot, cook the naan, one at a time. Brush each side of the prepared dough with melted butter, and place it in the hot skillet. Close the grill lid and cook for 2 minutes without opening the grill. Big bubbles should form. Then flip the dough and cook with the grill lid open for another 1 to 2 minutes, until lightly brown.

While the first naan cooks, melt the remaining butter in another bowl and stir in the Garlic Junky seasoning. Transfer the cooked naan to a platter and brush one side with the Garlic Junky butter. Cover loosely with a clean towel, and repeat the process with the remaining dough balls. Serve warm.

FAST HACK! If you don't have Garlic Junky seasoning, you can substitute the following blend for a copycat experience. Step one: Combine 3 minced garlic cloves, 1 tablespoon (18 g) of kosher salt, 1 tablespoon (10 g) of garlic powder and 1 tablespoon (7 g) of freshly ground black pepper and mix well. Step two: Get some Garlic Junky in your life!

SMOKY YORKSHIRE PUDDINGS

COOK TIME
15 minutes

YIELD
12 puddings (6 servings)

PELLET
Any

TECHNIQUE
Hot & Fast (page 19)

EQUIPMENT
Muffin pan or Yorkshire pudding pan

INGREDIENTS
3 large eggs, at room temperature

¾ cup (94 g) flour

¾ cup (180 ml) milk

¾ tsp kosher salt

¼ cup (60 ml) melted unsalted butter or rendered beef drippings (or a combination)

1 cup (113 g) shredded Gruyère or Swiss cheese (optional)

Traditionally served with roast beef during the holidays, these puffy, savory muffins are a perfect side to any grilled meat, including those special occasion meals and beyond. They truly are easy and tasty enough to enjoy any night of the week! If you are making them with a larger roast, such as the Prime Rib Roast (page 114), catch some of the flavorful drippings from the meat on the Traeger to use in the puddings, which makes them all the more decadent. You don't need a special pan for these—a regular-sized muffin pan will do the trick. If you'd like, you can add a little shredded cheese in the last moments of the cook to add an extra dimension to them.

Preheat your Traeger grill to 400°F (204°C). Place a muffin pan in the grill while it is heating up. Note: If you're cooking these Yorkshire puddings to accompany a prime rib, keep the grill running to cook the puddings after you've seared the roast, while it rests.

In a medium bowl, combine the eggs, flour, milk and salt, and whisk until just blended. Do not overmix. Allow the batter to sit at room temperature for 10 minutes while the pan heats up.

When ready to cook, carefully pour 1 teaspoon of butter in each cup of the preheated muffin pan and close the lid of the grill again for 3 minutes. After 3 minutes, carefully pour equal portions of the batter into each cup, filling halfway. Return the pan to the hot grill and cook for 10 to 15 minutes, until the puddings are puffed and golden brown. If desired, sprinkle with cheese and cook for 2 minutes more until the cheese is melted. Serve immediately.

FIRE-ROASTED JALAPEÑO POPPERS

COOK TIME
40 minutes

YIELD
24 poppers (8 servings)

PELLET
Any

TECHNIQUE
Outdoor Oven (page 21)

EQUIPMENT
Gloves (for handling the hot peppers)
Paring knife
Wire rack (optional)
Baking sheet lined with foil

INGREDIENTS
12 whole fresh jalapeños
1 tsp olive oil
1 (8-oz [227-g]) package of cream cheese, at room temperature
½ cup (57 g) shredded cheddar cheese
1 lb (454 g) bacon, cut in half widthwise
3 tbsp (43 g) Traeger Pork & Poultry rub
½ cup (120 ml) raspberry jam

I absolutely love poppers made on the grill, and they are always the appetizer my sister and my cousins request when they come over for dinner. These are stuffed with cream cheese, wrapped in bacon and grilled until the pepper is tender and the bacon is crispy. Serve with a bowl of raspberry jam, which will allow your guests to counteract the heat of the peppers if they get a particularly spicy one.

Preheat your Traeger grill to 300°F (149°C). Place the wire rack on the lined baking sheet (if using). Toss the whole jalapeños in olive oil and place them directly on the grates of the grill. Cook the peppers for about 20 minutes, until they're slightly browned and softened. Remove the peppers from the grill and allow them to cool until you can handle them.

Increase the grill temperature to 350°F (177°C). Wearing gloves and using a paring knife, slice the peppers in half lengthwise and scoop out the pith and seeds. You can leave some of the seeds if you want to serve hotter poppers. Combine the cream cheese and cheddar cheese in a bowl until just mixed. Then stuff each half-pepper with the cheese mixture (about 1 tablespoon [14 g] each). Wrap half of a bacon strip around each cheese-stuffed pepper half. Arrange the bacon-wrapped pepper halves on the foil-lined, grill-proof baking sheet, bacon seam side down. Use a toothpick to secure the bacon, if needed. Season the pepper halves with Traeger Pork & Poultry rub.

Cook the peppers in the grill for about 20 minutes, until the bacon is rendered and starting to crisp. Transfer to a platter and serve with the raspberry jam.

BACON CANDY

COOK TIME
20–25 minutes

YIELD
1 lb (454 g) bacon
(4–6 servings)

PELLET
Any

TECHNIQUE
Outdoor Oven (page 21)

EQUIPMENT
Grill-proof baking sheet
Wire rack (optional)
Parchment paper
Pastry brush

INGREDIENTS
1 lb (454 g) thick-cut bacon
2 tbsp (28 g) brown sugar
2 tbsp (30 ml) maple syrup
1 tbsp (5 g) red pepper flakes

I was first introduced to candied bacon as a topping on a burger at a local restaurant. While it's great as a burger topping, it can also be very versatile as a decadent appetizer or the central element to an amazing BLT. My recommendation is to make a full package of bacon, because there's a decent chance the cook won't get any if you have guests over!

Preheat your Traeger grill to 350°F (177°C). Line a baking sheet with parchment paper and place a wire rack on top, if using. Arrange the bacon slices on the prepared baking sheet.

In a small bowl, combine the brown sugar, maple syrup and red pepper flakes to make a thick paste. Using a pastry brush, spread the mixture evenly onto each slice of bacon.

Cook the bacon in the preheated grill for 15 to 25 minutes, checking frequently after 15 minutes, as it will cook quickly at the end. Transfer the bacon slices to a paper towel to drain. The bacon can be made ahead of time and kept at room temperature until ready to serve.

SMOKED ARTICHOKE DIP

COOK TIME
45 minutes

YIELD
6 servings

PELLET
Pecan

TECHNIQUE
Outdoor Oven (page 21)

EQUIPMENT
Grill-proof baking sheet
Grill-proof baking dish

INGREDIENTS
2 (14-oz [425-ml]) cans artichoke hearts packed in water, drained and quartered

1 (8-oz [227-g]) package of cream cheese, at room temperature

1 cup (240 ml) mayonnaise

2 green onions, thinly sliced

½ cup (50 g) plus 2 tbsp (13 g) grated Parmesan cheese, divided

½ cup (57 g) shredded Swiss cheese

Juice of ½ a lemon

2 tbsp (30 ml) hot sauce

Kosher salt

Freshly ground black pepper

Crackers, pita chips, toast rounds and/or fresh vegetables, for serving

Artichoke dip is a classic appetizer, and this recipe adds some distinctive smoky flavor from the Traeger grill to take it to the next level. We often assemble the dip ahead of time and put it in the fridge until a half hour before we're ready to serve it. Throw it in the grill to get hot and bubbly, and serve with crackers, sliced vegetables or toasted baguette rounds. Or it can even work as a tasty side to your main grilled meat with some crusty bread, bringing a balanced, tangy flavor to the meal.

Arrange the artichoke hearts in a single layer on a grill-proof baking sheet. Preheat your Traeger grill to 350°F (177°C), and place the baking sheet in the grill while it heats up, to to give the artichoke hearts some smoky flavor. After about 15 minutes, remove the baking sheet and roughly chop the artichoke hearts.

In a large bowl, combine the chopped artichoke hearts, cream cheese, mayonnaise, onions, ½ cup (50 g) of Parmesan cheese, Swiss cheese, lemon juice and hot sauce and mix well. Season with salt and pepper to taste and spread evenly in a grill-proof baking dish. Sprinkle the top with the remaining 2 tablespoons (13 g) of Parmesan cheese.

Bake the artichoke dip in the Traeger for 30 minutes, until it is hot and bubbly. Serve the dip with your choice of crackers, pita chips, toast rounds and/or fresh vegetables.

BAKED BRIE TWO WAYS

COOK TIME
20–30 minutes

YIELD
4–6 servings

PELLET
Any

TECHNIQUE
Outdoor Oven (page 21)

EQUIPMENT
Pink butcher paper or parchment paper

INGREDIENTS
1 small (7-oz [198-g]) wheel of brie cheese

1 package (8 slices) of thinly sliced prosciutto or 1 sheet of refrigerated puff pastry dough

3 tbsp (45 ml) raspberry jam, or pepper jam if you want something spicy

Crackers, crostini and/or apple slices, for serving

The first time I saw a recipe for brie baked in the Traeger, I knew I had to give it a try. If nothing else, it looked awesome. It turns out that it's not only a showstopper when you cut into it and the melted brie oozes out, but it also tastes absolutely delicious and comes together in nearly no time. It's so simple to prep—you can pop it in the grill just before you prep your main protein, especially one that benefits from a quick marinade like the Grilled Scallops in Citrus Mojo Marinade (page 88) or Marinated Skirt Steak (page 24). Enjoy snacking on the brie while your meat is grilling! We alternate our baked brie—sometimes in puff pastry and sometimes wrapped in prosciutto. The procedure is the same for either variation, so follow the directions below for the wrapping you prefer.

Preheat your Traeger grill to 350°F (177°C). While the grill preheats, prepare the cheese.

Begin by scoring the top of the cheese wheel with a sharp knife. Cut just deep enough to break through the rind without cutting into the cheesy center. On a piece of pink butcher paper or parchment paper, arrange the wrapping of your choice—either puff pastry or slices of prosciutto arranged in a star. The prosciutto option is pictured.

Place the scored brie in the center of the wrapping and top with heaping tablespoons of jam. Bring the edges of the wrapping together to fully enclose the cheese wheel.

Transfer the wrapped cheese on the paper to the center of the preheated grill and bake for 20 to 30 minutes, until the pastry is browned and/or the cheese feels soft. Arrange the baked brie on a platter with crackers, crostini and apple slices and cut it open with a very sharp knife to allow the cheese to ooze out.

WEEKNIGHT TRAEGER
DESSERTS

Until you've done it, baking in the Traeger seems like a wild idea. But remember, a Traeger grill is really a well-engineered wood-fired convection oven on wheels that sits in your backyard. The pellet hopper and auger produce consistent, predictable temperatures, and the barrel design ensures even heat distribution throughout the cook (or in this case, the bake!). Give these recipes a try to finish off your wood-fired dinners with an amazing and super easy sweet treat. You can assemble several of these desserts while your main dish is cooking, then pop them in the grill just before you sit down to eat. When dinner is done, dessert will be ready, hot off the grill!

SKILLET SPOON BROWNIES

COOK TIME
25 minutes

YIELD
8 servings

PELLET
Any

TECHNIQUE
Outdoor Oven (page 21)

EQUIPMENT
9-inch (23-cm) cast-iron skillet
Stand mixer, hand mixer or whisk

INGREDIENTS
Cooking spray
3 oz (85 g) unsweetened chocolate
8 tbsp (112 g) unsalted butter
4 large eggs, at room temperature
2 cups (400 g) white sugar
2 tsp (10 ml) vanilla extract
Pinch of kosher salt
1 cup (125 g) flour
½ cup (88 g) chocolate chips (optional)
1 tsp flaky sea salt, for topping (I like Jacobsen's Pure Flake Finishing Salt)

These homemade brownies are a superb treat when you want to cap off a great grilled dinner without much extra effort. The Traeger will impart a smoked flavor to the brownies that complements chocolate so well. And when your dinner guests see you pull this dessert off the grill, they'll definitely be asking for another invitation.

Preheat your Traeger grill to 350°F (177°C). Grease the bottom and sides of the cast-iron skillet with cooking spray.

In a saucepan, melt the unsweetened chocolate and butter together on the stove over very low heat for about 5 minutes. Don't walk away during this step. Stir the contents frequently, as the chocolate pieces will begin to melt quickly near the end. Be careful to avoid overcooking the chocolate. Remove the saucepan from the heat, and set it aside to cool slightly for 5 minutes.

Using a stand mixer, hand mixer or whisk, beat together the eggs, sugar, vanilla and salt for about 90 seconds, until well combined. Then slowly stir in the cooled chocolate-butter mixture until thoroughly combined. Stir in the flour and then the chocolate chips, if using.

Pour the batter into the prepared skillet and sprinkle the top with the sea salt. Transfer the skillet to the Traeger and bake for 20 minutes, until the center no longer looks runny. The brownies should be a bit gooey in the center, and cake-like around the edges. Allow to cool briefly, then serve by the spoonful.

BOURBON CHOCOLATE PECAN PIE

COOK TIME
1 hour 10 minutes

YIELD
Makes 1 (9-inch [23-cm]) pie
(8 servings)

PELLET
Pecan

TECHNIQUE
Outdoor Oven (page 21)

EQUIPMENT
Grill-proof baking sheet
9-inch (23-cm) glass pie plate

INGREDIENTS

2 cups (218 g) whole raw pecans

1 prepared refrigerated pie crust

3 large eggs, beaten

¾ cup (165 g) brown sugar

⅔ cup (160 ml) corn syrup

1 tsp vanilla

2 tbsp (28 g) unsalted butter, melted

3 tbsp (45 ml) bourbon whiskey

½ tsp kosher salt

1 cup (175 g) high-quality semisweet chocolate chips

2 tsp (12 g) flaky sea salt (I like Jacobsen's Pure Flake Finishing Salt)

This dish combines three of my favorite flavors with my favorite mode of cooking. A good bourbon, lots of high-quality chocolate and toasted pecans come together in a flaky pie crust as the perfect ending to a decadent meal. Any bourbon you have on hand will work, but I usually try to use something special to elevate it just a bit more. This pie can be assembled ahead of time, then baked and served warm, if you want to speed things up!

Preheat your Traeger grill to 375°F (191°C). Spread the pecans on a baking sheet in a single layer and place the sheet in the grill as it heats. Toast the pecans for about 10 minutes, until they are fragrant, being careful not to burn them. Remove the nuts from the grill and allow them to cool briefly. Roughly chop half of the toasted pecans, leaving the rest whole.

Press the refrigerated pie crust into a glass pie plate and crimp the edges. In a large bowl, combine the eggs, brown sugar, corn syrup, vanilla, butter, bourbon whiskey and kosher salt and mix well. Stir in all the pecans and the chocolate chips, and transfer the filling to the prepared pie plate.

Bake the pie in the grill for 45 to 55 minutes, until nearly set. Sprinkle the top with the sea salt and continue baking for another 5 minutes, until the center is set. Allow to cool briefly before serving. You can also cool it completely before serving, if desired.

UPSIDE-DOWN COBBLER

COOK TIME
50–55 minutes

YIELD
6 servings

PELLET
Any

TECHNIQUE
Outdoor Oven (page 21)

EQUIPMENT
Deep 9-inch (23-cm) ceramic pie plate or enameled Dutch oven

INGREDIENTS
4 tbsp (56 g) unsalted butter, cubed

½ cup (63 g) flour

½ cup (100 g) sugar

1 tsp baking powder

½ cup (120 ml) milk

2 cups (300 g) fruit, mixed with 2 tbsp (25 g) white sugar, if desired (we used 3 parts frozen sliced peaches and 1 part blackberries)

Whipped cream or ice cream, for serving

We use this recipe frequently in the summer months to highlight fresh local fruit. It's incredibly simple and delicious. Use whatever fruit you have access to—including frozen fruit (no need to defrost). It may seem backward to put the cobbler batter on the bottom of the dish, but it magically rises to the top as it cooks. This cobbler is delicious served hot, so pop it in the grill when you remove your entrée, and you'll have a new family-favorite dessert (and amazing leftovers for breakfast!).

Preheat your Traeger grill to 350°F (177°C). Scatter the butter in the bottom of your selected baking vessel. Place the dish in the grill while it preheats to melt the butter.

Meanwhile, in a medium bowl, combine the flour, sugar, baking powder and milk and mix well. Carefully remove the dish from the grill and pour the batter over the melted butter. Then pour the fruit on top of the batter. Place the dish back in the grill and bake for 50 to 55 minutes, until the top is golden brown. The cobbler can be served at any temperature—hot, room temperature or cold. Don't forget the ice cream or whipped cream!

APPLE TOFFEE GALETTE

COOK TIME
30 minutes

YIELD
1 (8-inch [20-cm]) galette
(8 servings)

PELLET
Any

TECHNIQUE
Outdoor Oven (page 21)

EQUIPMENT
Pink butcher paper or
parchment paper

Pastry brush

INGREDIENTS
1 prepared refrigerated pie
crust

2 cups (350 g) thinly sliced
apples (we like Honeycrisp
apples, as they are a little tart
and keep their shape when
baked)

2 tbsp (28 g) brown sugar

2 tbsp (16 g) cinnamon

1 tbsp (14 g) cold unsalted
butter, cut into small pieces

¼ cup (44 g) toffee bits

1 large egg, beaten

3 tbsp (43 g) turbinado or raw
sugar

A galette is just a flat, open-faced rustic pie. You can make galettes with a variety of savory and sweet fillings, but our favorite is a sweet galette filled with apples seasoned with cinnamon and bits of toffee. Make it quick and simple by using a store-bought pie crust and assemble it ahead of time to bake in the hot Traeger grill while you sit down to eat your main dish. Serve with a dollop of softly whipped cream or vanilla ice cream.

Preheat your Traeger grill to 400°F (204°C).

Unroll the pie crust in the center of a piece of parchment paper. In a medium bowl, combine the apples, brown sugar and cinnamon. Toss to coat and allow to sit for 5 minutes. The apples will let off a little liquid, which will help dissolve the sugar. Stir in the cold butter pieces and toffee bits, then mound the seasoned apples in the center of the prepared pie crust. Fold the edges of the crust around the pie, creating a flat, imperfect circle. Brush the crust with the beaten egg and sprinkle with the turbinado sugar.

Bake the galette in the Traeger for 30 minutes, rotating once halfway through until golden brown. Allow to cool briefly and cut into wedges to serve.

FAST HACKS! Another delicious variation on this recipe is to stuff the galette with stone fruit and berries, if they're in season. Thinly sliced peaches, plums or cherries can be substituted for the apples, and a handful of berries can replace the toffee and butter. Assemble the galette as noted above and bake until bubbly.

You can also make individual hand pies with these ingredients. Simply make smaller pie crusts, which you fold over the same way, and bake until golden.

SAUCES, BUTTERS & SALSAS

TO ELEVATE ANY DISH

This chapter provides recipe recommendations for BBQ sauces, compound butters, salsas and sauces that will complement your Traegered meals. Great grilled food shouldn't need sauce, in my opinion, but for the sauce-lovers among you, these recipes can augment and elevate an already great dish.

BBQ SAUCES

COOK TIME
10–25 minutes, depending on the variation

YIELD
1–2 cups (240–480 ml) of sauce

Excellent BBQ shouldn't need sauce, because you've cooked the meat well but not too long, which results in flavorful, moist meat. But sometimes a BBQ sauce really elevates a dish, and there are recipes throughout this book where sauces help take the cook to the next level. The six BBQ sauce recipes included in this section represent a variety of cuisines and flavors that will hopefully provide some inspiration as you experiment with your own variations. Mix and match these sauces with recipes throughout the book to customize your own unique flavor combinations!

KITCHEN SINK BBQ SAUCE

COOK TIME
10 minutes

INGREDIENTS
½ cup (120 ml) ketchup
¼ cup (60 ml) vinegar
¼ cup (60 ml) yellow mustard
¼ cup (55 g) brown sugar
¼ cup (60 ml) water
2 tbsp (30 ml) honey
1 tbsp (15 ml) Worcestershire sauce
½ tsp garlic powder
½ tsp onion powder
½ tsp ground mustard
½ tsp paprika

In a small saucepan, combine the ketchup, vinegar, yellow mustard, brown sugar, water, honey, Worcestershire sauce, garlic powder, onion powder, ground mustard and paprika. Bring to a simmer on the stove over low heat until slightly thickened, about 10 minutes. Adjust the seasoning to taste before serving. Use immediately or store in the fridge for up to a week.

ALABAMA WHITE SAUCE

COOK TIME
5 minutes

INGREDIENTS
1 cup (240 ml) mayonnaise

¼ cup (60 ml) apple cider vinegar

2 tbsp (28 g) brown sugar

1 tbsp (7 g) ground mustard

Juice of 1 lemon

2 tsp (10 ml) prepared horseradish

Kosher salt

Freshly ground black pepper

In a small bowl, whisk together the mayonnaise, vinegar, brown sugar, ground mustard, lemon juice and horseradish. Season with salt and pepper to taste (it should be quite tangy). Refrigerate until ready to use; the sauce can be stored in the fridge for up to a week.

ASIAN-STYLE BBQ SAUCE

COOK TIME
15 minutes

INGREDIENTS
½ cup (120 ml) prepared hoisin sauce

2 tbsp (30 ml) rice wine vinegar

1 tsp fish sauce

2 tbsp (30 ml) soy sauce

1 tbsp (15 ml) honey

¼ cup (40 g) minced red onion

2 garlic cloves, minced

1 tbsp (6 g) grated fresh ginger

1 tbsp (15 ml) sriracha hot sauce

¼ tsp Chinese five-spice powder

¼ cup (50 g) white sugar

In a bowl, combine the hoisin sauce, vinegar, fish sauce, soy sauce, honey, onion, garlic, ginger, sriracha and five-spice powder and mix well. In a saucepan or deep skillet, heat the sugar on the stove over low heat until it begins to melt and turn a dark caramel color, about 5 minutes. Carefully pour the hoisin mixture into the saucepan and stir constantly over low heat for 5 to 7 minutes until thickened. Allow the sauce to cool slightly before use. Use immediately or store in the fridge for up to a week.

MUSTARDY CAROLINA-STYLE BBQ SAUCE

COOK TIME

10 minutes

INGREDIENTS

1 cup (240 ml) yellow mustard

½ cup (120 ml) honey

⅓ cup (73 g) brown sugar

½ cup (120 ml) apple cider vinegar

2 tsp (10 ml) Worcestershire sauce

1 tbsp (15 ml) ketchup

1 tsp garlic powder

1 tsp onion powder

1 tsp cayenne pepper

1 tsp hot sauce

Kosher salt

Freshly ground black pepper

In a small saucepan, combine all the mustard, honey, brown sugar, vinegar, Worcestershire sauce, ketchup, garlic powder, onion powder, cayenne pepper and hot sauce and mix well. Simmer the sauce on the stove over low heat for 10 minutes, until slightly thickened. Season with salt and black pepper to taste. Use immediately or store in the fridge for up to a week.

SPICY CHIPOTLE BBQ SAUCE

COOK TIME

5–10 minutes

INGREDIENTS

2 cups (480 ml) tomato sauce

⅓ cup (80 ml) molasses

⅓ cup (80 ml) white vinegar

⅓ cup (80 ml) water

2 chipotle peppers in adobo sauce

2 tbsp (13 g) onion powder

1 tbsp (15 ml) Worcestershire sauce

1 tbsp (7 g) garlic powder

Kosher salt

Freshly ground black pepper

In a blender, combine the tomato sauce, molasses, white vinegar, water, chipotle peppers, onion powder, Worcestershire sauce and garlic powder and blend until smooth. Transfer the sauce to a small saucepan and simmer on the stove over low heat for 5 to 10 minutes, until slightly thickened. Season with salt and pepper to taste. Use immediately or store in the fridge for up to a week.

BOURBON BERRY BBQ SAUCE

COOK TIME
20–25 minutes

INGREDIENTS

1 tbsp (15 ml) cooking oil

½ cup (80 g) diced red onion

2 garlic cloves, minced

½ jalapeño pepper, diced (seeds removed if you want less heat)

½ pint (150 g) fresh or frozen blueberries, raspberries or blackberries (a combination would work great)

¾ cup (180 ml) ketchup

½ cup (110 g) brown sugar

½ cup (120 ml) apple cider vinegar

½ cup (120 ml) bourbon whiskey

Kosher salt

Freshly ground black pepper

In a saucepan, heat the oil over medium heat. Add the onion, garlic and jalapeño and cook for about 5 minutes, until softened. Stir in the berries, ketchup, brown sugar, vinegar and bourbon whiskey. Reduce the heat to low, and simmer for 5 to 10 minutes, until the berries begin to burst. Continue cooking, stirring frequently, until thickened, about 10 minutes longer.

If you want the sauce to be smooth, pour it into a blender and blend until smooth. Season with salt and pepper to taste and enjoy! Use immediately or store in the fridge for up to 4 days.

COMPOUND BUTTER

TOTAL TIME
5 minutes (plus 20 minutes to chill)

YIELD
4 tbsp (56 g) of flavored butter

INGREDIENTS
4 tbsp (56 g) unsalted butter, softened

Mix-ins of your choice (see Mix-In Combinations below)

Using a compound butter while grilling will soon become one of your favorite backyard BBQ secrets. The addition of a little fat and extra flavor to your cooks will elevate the dishes beyond your diners' expectations. As with the BBQ sauces, the flavors shared here are intended as inspiration, and I encourage you to experiment with other flavor combinations. Compound butters can be refrigerated for a week or more, so it's easy to always keep a few on hand for your cooks.

In a bowl, combine the softened butter and your choice of mix-in ingredients. Stir until thoroughly combined. Transfer the butter to a square of plastic wrap or parchment paper and roll into a log. Refrigerate for at least 20 minutes before slicing into discs to use.

MIX-IN COMBINATIONS

MY SPICEOLOGY SEASONING BLENDS (CHOOSE ONE)
4 tbsp (52 g) Garlic Junky seasoning

4 tbsp (46 g) Spicy Bloody Mary seasoning

4 tbsp (45 g) Double Smoke seasoning

CHIPOTLE
1 tbsp (17 g) finely chopped chipotle pepper in adobo sauce

½ tsp orange zest

½ tsp kosher salt

CITRUS
2 tbsp (12 g) citrus zest (orange, lemon, lime or grapefruit)

½ tsp kosher salt

MAPLE CINNAMON
2 tbsp (30 ml) maple syrup

1 tsp cinnamon

½ tsp kosher salt

PARMESAN HERB
3 tbsp (18 g) finely chopped fresh herbs (such as basil, parsley, thyme and rosemary)

2 tbsp (13 g) grated Parmesan cheese

1 garlic clove, minced

½ tsp kosher salt

HERB & MUSTARD
2 tbsp (30 ml) Dijon mustard

1 tbsp (1 g) finely chopped chives

½ tbsp (3 g) finely chopped tarragon

1 tbsp (1 g) finely chopped basil

½ tsp kosher salt

THAI
2 tbsp (32 g) Thai red curry paste

1 tsp Thai curry seasoning

2 garlic cloves, minced

spicy
Bloody
Mary ↓

Thai ↓

parmesan
herb ↓

herb
+
mustard ↙

maple
Cinnamon

Chipotle

Double
Smoke ↑

Garlic
Junky ↓

Citrus

SALSAS & SAUCES

COOK TIME
5–30 minutes, depending on
the variation

YIELD
1–2 cups (240–480 ml),
depending on the recipe

These non-BBQ sauce recipes offer other ways to elevate your amazing grilled meals. Many are mentioned in the cookbook, but I encourage you to be creative and mix and match to find your favorite combinations. And when in doubt, a perfectly grilled meat, a salsa and a great tortilla (I recommend Caramelo tortillas, which are available to order online) make for the perfect taco dinner!

CORN & POBLANO SALSA

TOTAL TIME
30 minutes

INGREDIENTS
2 ears of corn, shucked

2 whole, fresh poblano peppers

½ red onion, sliced into rounds

4 tbsp (60 ml) olive oil

Juice of 1 lime

1 tsp ground cumin

1 tsp garlic powder

Kosher salt

Freshly ground black pepper

Preheat your Traeger grill to 400°F (204°C). Once the grill is hot, roast the shucked corn, whole poblanos and onion slices for 12 minutes. Remove them from the grill and allow them to cool. Peel the skin off the poblanos (it should peel off easily). Cut the corn off the cobs and roughly chop the poblanos and red onion. Transfer the corn, poblanos and onion to a medium bowl, and add the olive oil, lime juice, cumin and garlic powder. Stir well to combine. Season with salt and pepper to taste.

CHIMICHURRI

TOTAL TIME
15 minutes

INGREDIENTS
1 bunch parsley, finely chopped

½ bunch cilantro, finely chopped

2 stems fresh oregano, leaves finely chopped

2 stems fresh thyme, leaves finely chopped

Juice of 2 lemons

1 small shallot, finely minced

2 garlic cloves, minced

1 small jalapeño, finely chopped (or substitute 2 tsp [4 g] red pepper flakes)

2 tbsp (30 ml) red wine vinegar

½ cup (120 ml) olive oil

Kosher salt

Freshly ground black pepper

In a small bowl, combine the parsley, cilantro, oregano, thyme, lemon juice, shallot, garlic, jalapeño, vinegar and olive oil and mix well. Season with salt and pepper to taste and add more olive oil if needed for your desired consistency. Set aside and serve at room temperature with grilled meat.

SMOKED PICO DE GALLO

TOTAL TIME
20 minutes

INGREDIENTS
3 large ripe tomatoes, diced
½ red onion, diced
1 jalapeño, diced
1 garlic clove, minced
1 tbsp (6 g) cumin
1 tsp dried oregano
Juice of 1 lime
4 tbsp (60 ml) olive oil
3 tbsp (45 ml) chopped cilantro
Kosher salt
Freshly ground black pepper

Preheat your Traeger grill to 225°F (107°C) and turn on the Super Smoke feature if your grill has it. Spread the tomatoes, onion and jalapeño on a grill-proof baking sheet. Smoke the vegetables in the preheated grill for 10 minutes. Transfer the tomatoes, onion and jalapeño to a medium bowl. Add the garlic, cumin, oregano, lime juice, olive oil and cilantro, and mix until thoroughly combined. Season with salt and pepper to taste and adjust the flavors as necessary.

SPINACH PESTO

TOTAL TIME
10 minutes

INGREDIENTS
1 lb (454 g) spinach
1 cup (20 g) basil leaves
4 garlic cloves
⅓ cup (80 ml) olive oil
⅓ cup (33 g) grated Parmesan cheese
Kosher salt
Freshly ground black pepper

In a saucepan, briefly steam the spinach in ½ inch (1.3 cm) of water over medium heat until just softened. Add the steamed spinach, basil, garlic, olive oil and cheese to a blender or food processor, and blend until smooth. Season with salt and pepper to taste. Serve alongside grilled fish, meat or veggies.

ACKNOWLEDGMENTS

While my name may be on the cover of this book, bringing this project to fruition was truly a team effort. From friends and family who have eaten through the good, the bad and the amazing things I've cooked on my Traeger to the team at Page Street Publishing who have so kindly guided me through this process, a debt of gratitude is owed to all. This Jew Can Que started casually when I got my first smoker as a wedding gift from colleagues, and I became intrigued (and then obsessed) with cooking anything and everything my wife and I could imagine. As the community around the brand has grown, I've been humbled by the people—both in the United States and internationally—who have rallied behind my work. I say it often, but the BBQ family is amazing, and I am lucky to get to be a part of it. To all my followers, thank you for your engagement and enthusiasm. There's a lot more to come.

As this project has progressed, I've had the opportunity to work with some amazing companies who have generously and enthusiastically supported the content that I create. Cooking all the dishes for this book in a five-day shoot was no small feat, and I am honored we were able to do so with the best companies behind me. Thank you to Traeger Grills for providing a product and a community that feels like family. Jeremy Andrus, Chad Ward, Tyler Stark, Krista Bava and Alex Noshirvan have been so supportive throughout, and I'm grateful to get to work with you all. To Snake River Farms, Salmon & Sable, Fulton Fish Company, Red Bird Farms, Superior Farms, Lobster Anywhere, Spiceology, Mac Cutting Boards, Caramelo Tortillas, Smithey Ironware and ThermoWorks, thank you for believing in me and what I do. Your generosity has been essential in my success.

Thanks to Sarah Monroe, my editor at Page Street, for her patient and thoughtful direction throughout the process. To Will Kiester, for his vision, and for bringing me into the Page Street family for this project. And to the rest of the Page Street team, for their remarkable work behind the scenes. I had the opportunity to work with Ken Goodman for this book, and he made the marathon photoshoot so rewarding. Your expertise as a chef and visionary photographer shines bright in these images, and I still find myself surprised that the food I cooked is represented on these plates.

To our friends—too numerous to name—thank you for jumping in at any step in this process to advise, edit, eat and help. Without the help of David Nelson each day of the photoshoot, there is no way we would have gotten the work done. Thank you, David, for your generosity and spirit. Thank you to our families for their support, excitement and patience as This Jew Can Que has gone from a mild joke to the real deal.

My wife, Isabel, to whom this book is dedicated. You're my right-hand woman, my best friend and my biggest cheerleader. I know that BBQ wasn't something you expected our life to revolve around, but you've been supportive beyond belief, and I'm grateful you're always a step ahead of me, discovering new recipes, keeping the pantry and fridge stocked, and always willing to hold the camera. Without your writing skills, organizational savvy and hard work, this book would never have gotten across the finish line.

And thank you to you, the readers, for getting this book and giving me a chance. I hope you find this book useful and inspiring for your own backyard cooks. Please tag me in the pictures of what you cook, and always feel free to drop me a note with questions, ideas and feedback. I look forward to hearing from you!

ABOUT THE AUTHOR

Adam McKenzie is a seventh-generation Colorado native and avid backyard grilling enthusiast. As the creator of the brand @ThisJewCanQue, Adam started his Instagram account as a means of sharing pictures of his emerging hobby with family and friends. Soon, however, his catchy moniker, content and recipes gained popularity, and by the end of 2020, he had more than 206,000 followers. The first to admit that he's a self-taught amateur, Adam loves the change of pace that cooking on his Traeger grills in his backyard brings to his life. By day, Adam is an elementary school STEM teacher, helping nearly 150 kids a day cultivate a love of learning through programming, engineering, game design and collaborative innovation.

Adam has partnered with dozens of companies over the years, writing recipes and creating content related to BBQ, including Traeger Grills, Snake River Farms and Buffalo Trace Distillery. In addition, he has a line of custom-branded seasonings through a partnership with Spiceology.

Adam cooks from his suburban Denver home that he shares with his wife, Isabel, and their goldendoodles, Halley and Maggie. When they're not planning content or entertaining friends and family in their backyard, he enjoys traveling, skiing, playing disc golf, building and collecting Legos and spending time with family.

He encourages you to reach out with questions, feedback and ideas, and he can't wait to hear from you!

  @ThisJewCanQue

thisjewcanque@gmail.com

www.jewcanque.com

INDEX